Divine Vision
William Blake in Felpham

by

James Martin Charlton

TSL Publications

First published in Great Britain in 2023
By TSL Publications, Rickmansworth

Copyright © 2023 James Martin Charlton.

ISBN: 978-1-915660-70-1

The right of James Martin Charlton. to be identified as the author of this work has been asserted by the author in accordance with the UK Copyright, Designs and Patents Act 1988.

All characters and events in this publication, other than those clearly in the public domain, are fictitious and any resemblance to actual persons, living or dead, is purely coincidental.

All rights reserved. No part of this publication may be reproduced,stored in a retrieval system or transmitted, in any form or by any means without the prior written permission of the publisher, nor be otherwise circulated in any form of binding or cover other than that in which it is published and without a similar condition being imposed on the subsequent buyer.

Cover design

Phillip Block

Author's Note

I first stumbled across the story of William Blake's period in Felpham whilst reading Northrop Frye's brilliant 1947 critical study of the poet and artist, *Fearful Symmetry*. Frye gives the following account,

> IN 1800, after Blake had been working for some time on The Four Zoas, he was offered a retreat at the village of Felpham in Sussex, by his patron and friend Hayley, himself a poet of sorts, who had also patronized Cowper. Blake was, like most major English writers, a born Cockney who quickly became miserable long outside London, but he naturally did not know that then, and went off very happily to live under Hayley's protection. It was almost the first "event" in a busy but very quiet life, and Blake planned that his stay in Felpham would be a "slumber" in a Beulah of dormant life during which he would gather together all his powers and concentrate them on clarifying the scheme of his epic and the technique of his engraving. He never ceased to speak of it as a slumber, but a quickly developing antagonism between his temperament and Hayley's soon made it a slumber full of nightmares: not an idyllic pastoral interlude or a sheltered hibernation, but an ordeal by fire, a temptation in a wilderness of fashionable smugness. (Frye, 1969, p. 313)

By the time of the move, Blake had already written his *Song of Innocence and Experience* (1794) and *The Marriage of Heaven and Hell* (1790–93), as well as developing a visual style as an artist which has led to him being considered one of Britain's greatest artists, but back then had barely made its mark beyond a small coterie of admirers. The fashionable sort considered him a proficient journeyman engraver, and it is in this role that he first met the very much more successful and wealthier poet and gentleman William Hayley. Hayley made Blake an offer he could not, but perhaps should have, refused:

to relocate to Felpham, a small seaside village in West Sussex, just outside of Bognor Regis. Blake was to undertake various commissions for Hayley, such was Blake's understanding, in any case. Hayley saw Blake more as a live-near amanuensis and described Blake in correspondence as "my secretary" (Ackroyd, 1995, p. 220).

Blake found himself illustrating Hayley's patently absurd collection of *Ballads founded on Anecdotes of Animals* (1805), which is akin to the great Russian filmmaking poet Andrei Tarkovsky being forced to make episodes of *Animals Do the Funniest Things*. Like Tarkovsky, Blake saw his artistic work as a mystical endeavour. Blake took it as his vocation to write epic poems, illustrated like medieval manuscripts, diagnosing and offering solutions to the spiritual problems of his fellow Britons. It was his job to tell the story of the fall and salvation of the Giant Albion. In Felpham, Blake was illustrating faithful Fido jumping into the jaws of a crocodile. Blake was, like the prophet Jonah, neglecting his divinely inspired mission; he had himself jumped into the blubbering jaws of whaley Hayley. His punishment was to suffer pangs of remorse and bouts of paranoia, to witness impotently the sickness of his beloved wife, and to find himself arrested when he ejected a drunken soldier who had wandered into the garden of the cottage at which Blake was living. Blake was tried for sedition, thankfully not found guilty, and returned to London chastened. In the increasingly penniless and obscure years that followed, he wrote the epics *Milton: A Poem in Two Books* (1804-10) and *Jerusalem: The Emanation of the Giant Albion* (1804-20). The lyric "And did those feet" – which is contained within the preface to Milton but which we now know best as the hymn Jerusalem – was written after a divine vision in that very Felpham cottage garden. The more I read about it, the more it seemed to me that the story had it all – temptation, high stakes, a trial, revelation and restoration. I determined to turn it into a play.

I secured a grant from the Peggy Ramsay Foundation, having been kindly recommended by the theatre producer Michael Codron, and spent weeks in the British Library researching the play. I read countless critical studies and biographies of Blake, as well as familiarising myself with the man's complete oeuvre. Because John Milton was such an important figure to Blake at this time, he needed to become a character in the play, and so I spent as much time getting to know the author of *Paradise Lost*.

I also became extremely familiar with William Hayley, Esq. Peter Ackroyd describes Hayley's autobiography as "one of the most inadvertently comic narratives of the early nineteenth century (...) written in an ornate and convoluted prose in which he refers to himself throughout as 'Hayley' or 'the Poet'." Morchard Bishop's rollicking and ultimately poignant biography (1951) supplied me with more than I ever needed to know about this now obscure figure, who was offered but turned down the post of Poet Laureate in his day. I determined to capture the full comic grotesquery and pomposity of Hayley in the play, but also strove to treat him as kindly as I could. At times in his writing, Blake conflates Hayley with Satan, but Blake's vision finally led him to see that "I in my Selfhood am that Satan" (Blake & Ostriker, 1977, p. 540). Blake took responsibility for his own mistakes as he turned his life in the direction that he determined Jesus, whom he considered God, wanted him to go. My play is a narrative ultimately of reconciliation, including self-reconciliation and reconciliation with the divine, which may amount to the same thing.

At one point in my research, I perused a British Library copy of Hayley's once-famous poem *The Triumphs of Temper* (1781). In it was written a dedication from the author to one Mrs Blake. This edition was given from the hands of my antagonist to the hands of Catherine, my lead female character, and this copy of the book must surely have been handled by Blake himself. I felt that the baton of writing this story as a play had been handed to me. I hope that I have done the story, as complex, singular and universal as it is, some justice. My agent thought it my best play.

Despite this, *Divine Vision* did not see a full production at the time. I staged a reading at Swedenborg Hall, and producers toyed with it and me; the then literary manager of the RSC, Paul Sirett, passed it amongst the company's directors, none of whom went for it. The failure of the play to reach production was a source of the greatest sorrow in my writing career, which – despite some notable triumphs – has hardly been short of sorrows. Nevertheless, it now belatedly but joyously reaches publication, for which I am eternally grateful to TSL Publications and their director Dr Anne Samson.

Divine Vision now lays in your hands, to read and perhaps even to produce. Then William and Catherine Blake, John Milton, the drunken soldier and that extraordinary fellow William Hayley can walk the stage as I planned, re-enacting the timeless story of a prophet's nightmarish mistake in neglecting his mission, his sufferings in so doing, and his redemption and resurrection to the eternal life of fame that is forever his.

JMC, June 2023

Select Bibliography

Ackroyd, P. (1995). *Blake*. London: Sinclair-Stevenson.

Bishop, M. (1951). *Blake's Hayley: The Life, Works, and Friendships of William Hayley.* London: Gollanez.

Blake, W., & Ostriker, A. (1977). *The Complete Poems.* London: Penguin Books.

Frye, N. (1969). *Fearful Symmetry: A Study of William Blake.* Princeton: Princeton University Press.

FIGURES IN THE DRAMA

WILLIAM BLAKE, *a prophet.*

CATHERINE BLAKE, *his wife.*

JOHN MILTON, *a puritan poet.*

ROBERT, *a student of art.*

WILLIAM HAYLEY, *a poet and patron.*

MARY, *a country maid.*

LADY BATHURST, *an aristocrat.*

SKOLFIELD, *a soldier.*

SAMUEL ROSE, *an advocate.*

THE LAMB OF GOD, *a Divine Vision.*

The play takes place in London and Felpham in the years 1800-1803.

Doubling of performers

JOHN MILTON and SKOLFIELD can be played by the same actor.

ROBERT the student, SAMUEL ROSE and THE LAMB can also share a performer.

Therefore, the play requires a cast of 7 actors.

"And Jacob sod pottage: and Esau came from the field, and he was faint:

And Esau said to Jacob, Feed me, I pray thee, with that same red pottage; for I am faint: therefore was his name called Edom.

And Jacob said, Sell me this day thy birthright.

And Esau said, Behold, I am at the point to die: and what profit shall this birthright do to me?

And Jacob said, Swear to me this day; and he sware unto him; and he sold his birthright unto Jacob.

Then Jacob gave Esau bread and pottage of lentiles; and he did eat and drink, and rose up, and went his way: thus Esau despised his birthright."

>*Genesis*,
>Chapter 25, verses 29:34.

"Again, the devil taketh him up into an exceeding high mountain, and showeth him all the kingdoms of the world; and the glory of them;

And saith unto him, All these things will I give thee, if thou wilt fall down and worship me.

Then saith Jesus unto him, Get thee hence, Satan: for it is written, Thou shalt worship the Lord thy God, and him only thou shalt serve.

Then the devil leaveth him, and, behold, angels came and ministered unto him."

>*The Gospel According to Saint Matthew*,
>Chapter 4, verses 8-11.

"I in my Selfhood am that Satan: I am that Evil One!"

>William Blake, *Milton*.

ACT ONE
SCENE ONE

(A man stands in a doorway, emerging from darkness to Light.)

BLAKE: I had terrible trouble getting here. I traversed a universe of chaos. Wandering perplexed and moping down mazes of harshness with faces who I mark mask lives which are made up of worrying, fearing, and hoping, without always knowing what they do hope for. The ruined children of Jerusalem lost in humanity's fallen world. But.

I see the divine vision clearly. A paradise of fellowship, creativity, and love. Each of us shining, constantly making manifest the glories of God. TOGETHER ONE GREAT ETERNAL HUMANITY! But. We fall into division. We die. We shall be redeemed and resurrected to eternal life. I see it all and so I have my mission: telling this tale in an epic poem. A task which I am striving to fulfil. Meanwhile barely eking a living. But. Keeping that vision alive for you.

(We hear and then see CATHERINE BLAKE *singing one of her husband's songs as a small engraver's shop comes to light,* WILLIAM BLAKE *framed in the doorway.)*

CATHERINE: "And so Tom awoke; and we rose in the dark,
And got with our bags and our brushes to work,
Tho' the morning was cold, Tom was happy and warm,
So if all do their duty, they need not fear harm."

(BLAKE *comes through the door and kisses* CATHERINE.)

CATHERINE: Did you get it?

BLAKE: I did.

CATHERINE: How much?

BLAKE: Ten shillings ten pence.

CATHERINE: The poor rate's due Monday.

BLAKE: I'm aware.

(*Pause*.)

No need to fret about it.

CATHERINE: I get nervous.

BLAKE: All shall be well, and all manner of things shall be (CATHERINE... *gives him a look – "don't kid me".* BLAKE *sits at his desk and prepares to work.* CATHERINE *plucks up the courage*.)

CATHERINE: There's something else. Best to tell you. You'll only look out the back and see...

BLAKE: What?

CATHERINE: He's got that boy of his chained in the yard again.

(BLAKE *throws his pencil down*.)

No Will! Leave it.

BLAKE: I told that knave of a circus-owner, if he insists on keeping that child bound out in the wind and the rain, he'll have me to bandy fists with!

CATHERINE: It's warm today. The lad grins. He looks hearty.

BLAKE: The lad is an idiot.

CATHERINE: There'll just be one big row and for a few days he'll give the boy freedom. Then his heart hardens and the boy's back out. So, you give Astley two lovely

	black eyes, and he has you beaten by Atlas his strong man. And the boy never gets free, does he?
BLAKE:	Stop! That tale…
CATHERINE:	What?
BLAKE:	The world's cycles of violence revolving.

(BLAKE *slumps.*)

I am Atlas. Shouldering the weight of the world. Under standing.

(CATHERINE *turns away, sighing. He looks forward, rapt.*)

My tiny struggle is but a drop in time's ocean. Across the waters my fellow countrymen war against their brothers as the universal fraternity fades into nonentity. My nation's manufacturing industries have exchanged the arts of life for death. Ploughshares are beat into swords and pruning hooks turn spears. Youth is educated to ignorance. Thousands of sons fall in Netherlands battles and England oppresses the Irish, exploits flesh of Africans as a commodity, and encourages the counter-revolutionary French. The soul of an honest man sickens but speaking out courts a noose. Years ago, the Eternal Great Humanity Divine opened his heavens, showed me visions, the spirit entered, called me for a saint in these latter times. All was revealed – four living creatures – a voice:

VOICE:	"COPY THIS SCROLL!"
BLAKE:	Which I strive to do in my epics which I take to a desolate marketplace where none comes to buy. Hardly now hearing the Lord's voice above the

battle's din. Thames' dark waters lave through a London in which I'm drowning.

(CATHERINE *has got the gist of his mood.*)

CATHERINE: I thought you said, "don't worry".

BLAKE: Having allowed myself a few moments dirge-like lamentation for humanity's fallen state and all my woes, I feel life pulsing through me again and gladly get on with work.

(BLAKE *sets to work again.*)

CATHERINE: What are you working on?

BLAKE: The "Paradise Lost" illustrations.

CATHERINE: Getting paid for doing work you love. How many can say that?

BLAKE: This is work to perform with enthusiasm.

CATHERINE: Bit too much enthusiasm sometimes. Rows you have with that Milton.

BLAKE: Hush! Don't name him. You know how what he's like. First chance he gets he's here, causing a rumpus. I simply wish to sit and draw in peace.

(*But* JOHN MILTON *has appeared. An old, imposing, blind Puritan, his face is a stony mask.*)

MILTON: I come not to bring peace but a sword!

BLAKE: Talk of the devil.

CATHERINE: He's here?

BLAKE: He's arrived.

MILTON: How dare ye, with sharp impudence, refer unto me as to that dweller in rank shitten darkness, Satan, that arch fallen one.

BLAKE: Oh yes, Johnny-boy Milton is here, with his paragraph-long sentences. He's not happy.

MILTON: I am a soul in bliss.

BLAKE: Looks like it.

MILTON: And wherefore should I not be? Having led through my threescore years and six span, in this wretched vale of disappointment and tears...

BLAKE: Get on with it.

MILTON: ...a pure and virtuous life.

BLAKE: Never once committing a sin.

MILTON: My soul is white as linen.

BLAKE: Quite the Lady.

MILTON: I've instructed you, do not call me that.

BLAKE: I thought you were for freedom of speech?

MILTON: Liberty yea, not license.

(MILTON *looks at the drawing* BLAKE *is working on.*)

What be this?

BLAKE: One of my illustrations to your poem. Raphael descending into Paradise. Catherine, look at this...

CATHERINE: Don't drag me into it. I don't want to be bothered with the ins and outs of it all.

BLAKE: These arguments matter to all! Who is this in the sky?

CATHERINE: God I suppose.

MILTON: Great Lord Almighty!

BLAKE: How does he appear?

CATHERINE: A right gloomy old grey beard.

MILTON:	All-wise creator of Heaven and Earth.
BLAKE:	A bat-shaped and bodiless malice casting his malevolence down.
MILTON:	Blasphemous felon.
BLAKE:	Yes, he is.
MILTON:	Thou!
BLAKE:	(*To* CATHERINE) Now have a gander at these two. Eve and Adam. What do you see?
CATHERINE:	Happy couple, ain't they? At ease. In love. In the noddy.
BLAKE:	"...erect and tall / Godlike erect, with naked honour clad / In naked majesty."
MILTON:	/ "In naked majesty."
BLAKE:	Your own words.
CATHERINE:	Godlike erect?
BLAKE:	Walking through paradise with the horn.
CATHERINE:	Ooh, stop it. You'll get me all hot.
MILTON:	Porks savour the farm filth.
BLAKE:	There's nothing filthy about love. Your faults are glaring. Your God is of worse character than the humans he creates. What good does such divine vision do us? What we need is a friend and not a belligerent old Dad. (*He sings*) Old nobodaddy on high, Belches and farts and sighs. What a bloody disgrace To give God your own ugly face! (BLAKE *and* CATHERINE *laugh*.)

There must be something more human behind this stony old mask...

(BLAKE *attempts to rip off* MILTON's *Puritan mask, but* MILTON *evades him.*)

MILTON: I did not come here to be mocked.

BLAKE: You get enough of that in Heaven.

MILTON: Ignorant wretch.

(BLAKE *blows a rasp at* MILTON, *who disappears.* BLAKE *sinks back into his seat.*)

CATHERINE: Has he gone?

BLAKE: Yes. And routed.

CATHERINE: You always get so worked up with him. Ain't he your big inspiration?

BLAKE: He is full of errors. That countenance of stone...

(BLAKE *gets down to work again and* CATHERINE *wanders back to her spinning wheel but just as they knuckle down to it the front door opens and a very sickly-looking young student –* ROBERT *– stands there.*)

ROBERT: Mister and Missus Blake.

CATHERINE: Robert!

BLAKE: Come in Rob!

(ROBERT *staggers in.* CATHERINE *pulls a chair out and* BLAKE *helps* ROBERT *to sit.*)

ROBERT: I hope it is not inconvenient.

BLAKE: Not a blot.

(BLAKE *rubs* ROBERT's *hand.*)

By the love of God, you're freezing. Come on Catherine, the lad wants warmth!

(CATHERINE *takes* ROBERT's *other hand and rubs it.*)

CATHERINE: Poor child. Frozen stiff!

ROBERT: Too much fussing.

BLAKE: Never enough fussing!

(BLAKE *and* CATHERINE *love* ROBERT. *They perch around him.*)

It's been ages.

CATHERINE: We was getting worried.

BLAKE: Worried stiff.

ROBERT: I've barely been out of my room. I haven't even been attending my studies.

BLAKE: Your health?

ROBERT: (*Nods*) My health.

CATHERINE: He's not eating enough. Feel him. Feel you! Thin as a bone. I won't have it. Whilst you're in my house, you'll eat something.

ROBERT: No need...

CATHERINE: Tell him, Mister Blake.

BLAKE: Best not to scorn her cooking, Rob.

CATHERINE: Answer me: are you cold?

ROBERT: I am.

CATHERINE: And are you hungry?

ROBERT: Ravening.

CATHERINE: The truth is out!

BLAKE: It never likes skulking.

CATHERINE: Some broth for our guest coming.

(CATHERINE *rises and exits to the kitchen.* BLAKE *looks at* ROBERT, *smiling.*)

BLAKE: You're a very sweet person to help her feel wanted this way. She loves to feel useful.

ROBERT: I myself am useless.

BLAKE: You brighten our lives with your very presence. Have you been feeling very ill?

ROBERT: I get no heat and agues shake me. At night sweat turns my bed to the sea. I twist and flounder and fetch precious little sleep.

BLAKE: I shall redouble my prayers for you.

ROBERT: I fear that's no use.

BLAKE: Let not a fever shake your faith, Rob – though it shakes your bones as a carriage over cobblestones.

ROBERT: My faith is thoroughly shaken.

BLAKE: Don't allow that decline to continue. Yes, you're illness-buffeted nightly but faith is the lighthouse will help you not sink.

ROBERT: It is foolish to hope in vain.

BLAKE: Who says?

ROBERT: My physician fears the worst.

BLAKE: No!

(CATHERINE *re-enters with a bowl of steaming broth.*)

CATHERINE: Mister Blake, why do you cry out thus?

(*To* ROBERT) Here love: a good bowl of broth.

ROBERT: Thank you.

(CATHERINE *puts the bowl before* ROBERT *and begins feeding him with a spoon.*)

BLAKE: It's Robert's physician.

CATHERINE: What about him?

ROBERT: He says there's no hope.

CATHERINE: No!

BLAKE: You see. It makes you cry out.

CATHERINE: There's always hope.

ROBERT: Not when nature insists otherwise.

BLAKE: "Nature." Nature! I've wrestled with nature as Jacob wrestled God's angel. "Nature"? Custom they mean! They deal in the ratio of things known, which is never as much as will be known. Nature – a world out there. Separate. Separate? WHERE?

I have never found anything which exists outside of my mind and as my mind is infinite, an infinity of things can happen. Miracles happen in infinite minds.

ROBERT: I fear you cannot prove this.

BLAKE: Listen to me, Robert. Listen to me with the gates of your mind wide open and your perception cleansed for I will now impart to you the Truth:

God will give you whatever you ask of Him. All He asks is that you Believe.

ROBERT: I doubt this.

BLAKE: Did the woman who touched the hem of His garment doubt? A woman who'd suffered years and been under many physicians and spent every penny she had, and they nothing bettered her, but she grew worse. She touched Him and she was cured.

ROBERT: I wish I could believe.

BLAKE: I have seen your drawings. That first time we saw you with your portfolio, I told Cate: "fetch him in."

CATHERINE: We knew there was something about you.

BLAKE: Your work was a revelation. Firm, determinate outlines. Not the hand of a plagiary who works only from memory – for then we should have seen only clumsy indefinite meaningless blots. So many artists rub out most of their lines as their progress is that of a blind man groping his way all unknowing. You know what you do. You have that greatest of blessings: a strong imagination. Do you hold that the loving father who gave you this gift will not give you more time to use it if asked?

He does not give us a stone for bread. He gives us no serpent for sustenance. He gives us life, light, eternal well-being. He'll give these things to you. Rob – ask him. Do.

ROBERT: The world would be so fine if that were true. I've an appointment.

BLAKE: And I must get working.

ROBERT: I'm sorry to have interrupted...

BLAKE: Nonsense! It's always a joy to see you.

(BLAKE *hugs* ROBERT.)

I know I go wild. I know I go on. When spirit insists, it must come pouring.

CATHERINE: When the spirit moves him, he raves!

(*The three of them laugh.*)

I hope you enjoyed the broth.

ROBERT: Delicious.

BLAKE: She has her uses.

CATHERINE:	Oh, do I?
BLAKE:	She is infinitely gifted!
CATHERINE:	That's better.
BLAKE:	(*To* ROBERT) Visit us more often.
ROBERT:	I'll try.
BLAKE:	Don't you go believing those doctors.
ROBERT:	We'll see.
CATHERINE:	And eat. Come here and eat.
ROBERT:	I shall. Farewell.
BLAKE:	God bless you.
CATHERINE:	God bless you. |//
(ROBERT THE STUDENT *exits to the street.*

WILLIAM *and* CATHERINE BLAKE *watch and wave at him as he departs down the street then turn back into their shop.*)

CATHERINE:	Not well at all.
BLAKE:	Physicians. They might say "I cannot cure you." Allow that the failing is theirs. But to say "incurable." They sin against spirit.
CATHERINE:	Don't get in a state.
BLAKE:	Quaint his name is Robert.
CATHERINE:	I know it reminds you.
BLAKE:	My brother chose to go. This filthy world wasn't worthy of him. I wish he'd not left me behind.

(*Pause.*)

CATHERINE:	I have a peck of shopping to do. Some money?
WILLIAM:	Here you are.

(BLAKE *hands some coins to* CATHERINE.)

	Enough?
CATHERINE:	(*Nods*) Get some bread and milk.

(CATHERINE *puts a coat on*.)

Shan't be long.

BLAKE: I'll work.

(*Exit* CATHERINE *to the street.*

BLAKE *walks slowly to his desk and sits. He picks up his pencil – is about to draw – then puts it down.*)

Not long go – when I was young – popular opinion had begun believing that this world could be our Paradise. The reign of priest and tyrants done. Liberty of mind and body. All of God's children Earth's owners.

Folk rushed together in mass demonstrations. Brotherly correspondence began. Thousands in fields together did stand. I myself took my place in the crowd as we stormed along Long Acre yelling "NO POPERY!" The fortress was burned, and the prisoners set free.

(JOHN MILTON *appears. He is less stony and can see.*

His eyes are alight.)

MILTON: Methought I saw in my mind a noble and puissant nation rousing herself like a strong man after sleep and shaking her invincible locks, an eagle mewing her mighty youth and kindling her undazzled eyes at the full midday beam.

BLAKE: That's the Spirit! Our brothers over the sea achieved much, taking up arms against their oppressor and declaring society's governing precepts as "Liberty! Equality! Fraternity!"

MILTON: We led our Stuart king to atonement.

BLAKE: Uneasy...

MILTON: We set the world a shining example of a nation pledged to Liberty!

BLAKE: The door slams shut again. The dragon Pitt sets his six —

MILTON: Six?

BLAKE: (*Nods*) Six Acts against combination, stopping all fraternal Union. The beauteous Gallic Samson turns to a form reptilian, bannered under her bony war lord, Napoleon. Leviathan and Behemoth fight to the death. Youth rots on the fields of Europe.

MILTON: I had thought the Apocalypse immanent. God's Millennium. Eschaton Now.

BLAKE: It didn't happen tho', did it, John?

(*During the following,* MILTON's *eyes begin to close.*)

MILTON: Our Chief of Men protected us from Liberty. The sun went out. My eyes turned blind. The fools danced to the starting place. "Fetch us a captain back for Egypt."

(MILTON *is blind and old again.*)

BLAKE: Revolution. Youth springs out from the old wintry loins and revolves the way back to his forebear's condition.

MILTON: I call to the rocks! O earth, earth, earth!

BLAKE: Who hears the prophet calling?

(MILTON *disappears.* BLAKE *is alone.*)

I am alone in history, with the ancient footsteps fading...

(Of a sudden the street door is flung open and WILLIAM HAYLEY, a large man in his fifties, stands framed in the doorway. He has a walking stick in one hand and an umbrella in the other. HAYLEY peers in myopically.)

HAYLEY: Pray tell me, sir, has this faltering pilgrim found himself at the correct address: the residence of that interesting engraver ennobling the appellation Blake?

BLAKE: Mister Hayley!

HAYLEY: Ah, 'tis thee!

BLAKE: Do come in sir.

(BLAKE rushes to HAYLEY and escorts him in. HAYLEY walks with a pronounced limp.)

HAYLEY: A most jungle-reminiscent district of the Capital doth good Blake reside. This hermit has been tottering it for hours, sadly hampered as you are well aware by a vision increasingly impaired. He almost despaired of discovering you.

BLAKE: Mister Hayley has honoured me before...

HAYLEY: Always escorted, sir. Always led. Today the hermit is unaccompanied.

BLAKE: Do sit down sir.

HAYLEY: Most welcome suggestion.

(HAYLEY sits.)

Your visitor's legs do ache as if he had walked the route of the Canterbury Miller. Eye this wretch before you, Blake! Allow him into your mind. Just as you have led him into your humble abode.

BLAKE: Mister Hayley has a secure place within my consciousness.

HAYLEY: What sweet kindness! But the Hayley before you today is a man transfigured by grief.

BLAKE: I'm sorry to hear that.

HAYLEY: His suffering Thomas Alfonso is no more.

(HAYLEY *begins to weep*.)

BLAKE: Mister... William... My heart is thine.

(BLAKE *holds* HAYLEY's *hand tenderly*.)

HAYLEY: A bereaved father thanks thee.

(*Pause*.)

'Twas a blessed release. How grieved this father had been to see him so tortured over these past years. A pitiable decline to witness: promising youth to cripple now corse.

BLAKE: An angel has departed us.

HAYLEY: That is the fact of it!

BLAKE: This life is ever a valley of joy and misery mixed.

HAYLEY: Too true.

BLAKE: Thirteen years ago, I lost a brother. The closest companion I've ever known.

HAYLEY: How to surmount these mammoth trials?

BLAKE: No loved one ever is lost. I have many hours conversed with my Robert in spirit and must confess to seeing him often in regions of Imagination.

HAYLEY: How quaint.

BLAKE: The ruins of time build mansions in Eternity. If we'd truly see what surrounds us, we'd know we are the constant companions of angels.

HAYLEY: Dearest friend!

(HAYLEY *hugs* BLAKE *very close*.)

You penetrate the heart of a hermit. Thomas Alfonso – that son believed lost – discovered again in Forever. A father thanks you for the directions to his lost loved one.

(HAYLEY *produces a book*.)

Let him present you a gift.

BLAKE: No need sir.

HAYLEY: This tome is Hayley's masterpiece. His "Triumphs of Temper". You have perused?

BLAKE: I have always meant to.

HAYLEY: Hayley's fortune this poem is. Enormous sales these twenty years. A tale it is concerning one Serena, a fascinating maid who undergoes many a trying test – for she is forever tempted to enter the gates of Spleen. Spleen, sir. Spleen! That spectre of peevish petulance which is society's greatest foe.

BLAKE: Astonishing subject.

HAYLEY: Its bard has always held so. But this is a tale in which Spleen triumphs not. Temper triumphs! Hence yon title. The author presents his present to you.

BLAKE: I sincerely thank him.

HAYLEY: Those most sincere thanks will grow when you discover a thus far clandestine secret: this very

	copy of "The Triumphs" belonged to the author's dear departed angel son.
BLAKE:	I do not deserve...
HAYLEY:	None deserves it more than thou who hast shown one dwelling in despair's darkness hope's illume. Let the work's genius inscribe...
	(HAYLEY *snatches the book from* BLAKE.)
BLAKE:	Most kind.
	(HAYLEY *produces a pen and considers*.)
HAYLEY:	Now what...? Ah yes! Let's see...
	(HAYLEY *writes in the book*.)
	"Accept, my gentle visionary Blake, Whose thoughts are fanciful and kindly mild, Accept, and fondly keep for friendship's sake, This favoured vision, my poetic child."
	(BLAKE *reaches for the book*.)
BLAKE:	You are too generous.
HAYLEY:	The muse has not winged off yet.
	(HAYLEY *writes on*.)
	"Rich in more grace than fancy ever won, To thy most tender mind this book will be, For it belonged to my departed son, So from an angel it descends to thee."
	(HAYLEY *presents the book to* BLAKE.)
BLAKE:	I shall treasure it ever.
HAYLEY:	'Tis a fine read. Now business. The hermit did not make his weary way through these rancorous environs for the sheer joyous hell of it! He has a bugbear.

BLAKE: Sir, what?

HAYLEY: Your engraving of the departed one.

(*Suddenly angry*) Sir, may a humble employer point out that your work has a great and radical defect? The etching has a head some three years older than on the medallion I gave you. The features have lost the lively juvenility of sixteen and appear elongated and sedate. You, sir, have failed egregiously! Do you think that paternal affection would let a portrait of his child with a heavy sullen sulky face go before the public?

BLAKE: I have hopelessly erred.

HAYLEY: Would the artist allow a mere amateur to make a suggestion? Would it not give the engraving a somewhat better appearance if you were to shorten the space between the nose and the upper lip more? Perhaps presenting the mouth open, in the act of speaking, which appears to this beholder – half-blind though he be – to be the expression on the medallion!

BLAKE: I shall strive to do so.

HAYLEY: You will?

(*Cries out*) Oh! A sufferer with a pressing pain of a sudden upon his bladder must use your convenience. Where be it?

BLAKE: In the back yard.

HAYLEY: Excuse a piss-requiring hermit.

(BLAKE *helps* HAYLEY *towards the kitchen.* HAYLEY *goes off.* BLAKE *staggers back into the room.* BLAKE *falls to his knees as he remembers something.*)

BLAKE:	Walking musing on Peckham Rye. I glance up at a tree often passed by. Glittering things in that tree. The wings of angels! I see their faces. How they beam. They smile and waft enormous wings. I feel that gliding deep in my stomach. I taste a Celestial air déjà vu. I hear a soaring as they start a-flying and up and up and UP and they're gone. I told my Father I saw angels. He threatened to beat me. I refused to be beat! Says he, "seeing angels, Will, will bring you only ignominy." Earthly ignominy is Heaven's laurel crown. I hate fathers! (BLAKE *gets off his knees, determined to confront* HAYLEY. HAYLEY *enters*.)
HAYLEY:	The hermit owes you an apology.
BLAKE:	Sir?
	(HAYLEY *limps to* BLAKE.)
HAYLEY:	He worries that he perhaps has been harsh. Perchance tempted he was unto Spleen. It is the still-sore loss of his beloved cripple. Hayley is sure you will forgive him.
BLAKE:	Of course, sir. (HAYLEY *beams*.) I can well recall my angers when Robert died. Even now when the sorrow grabs me it causes me pain which prompts irritability.
HAYLEY:	A kind and condoning visionary. Hayley loved his promising Thomas. Never would he suffer the boy to be beat. Hayley himself was whacked as a child. He nearly died and when he survived, doctors thought he'd been left an idiot.

BLAKE: We are brothers who've suffered at the hands of the cruel. You were a generous, loving father to Thomas.

HAYLEY: Consoling Blake.

(HAYLEY *strokes* BLAKE's *cheek*.)

Have you no other close relation of the masculine sex?

BLAKE: My other brothers are worldly men.

HAYLEY: Poor solitary. You know that one of the hermit's greatest prides was his bosom companionship to that interesting sufferer, Cowper.

BLAKE: A privilege sir, I am sure.

HAYLEY: Alas the cause of yet more sorrow, as that genius has also recently died. The hermit will keep him alive – just as he will keep alive his own dear son angel – for the hermit has two important projects about to commence, don't you know?

(*Pause.*)

BLAKE: (*Eventually*) And what projects are they, sir?

HAYLEY: Kind of you to take an interest! Hayley is intent upon two "Lives". One of his departed Thomas Alfonso and the other of that aforesaid Cowper.

BLAKE: Exciting projects indeed sir.

HAYLEY: Inspiration's call! Hayley's "Life of Cowper" needs illustrations and whom better to engrave the plates than that other very interesting artist whose name is... enthusiastic Blake!

BLAKE: I should be honoured sir.

HAYLEY: The job is thine! The work will need thee to be at the constant side of Hayley. Another interesting

	suggestion therefore! Why not move, with your good lady, down to that secluded village whereat the hermit hides from Man. Sweet Felpham! A great opportunity for you.
BLAKE:	Sir...
HAYLEY:	The Sussex gentry are big appreciators of the Arts and Hayley has no small influence amongst them. Introductions can be arranged... How does your business in London?
BLAKE:	It does not prosper.
HAYLEY:	You've nothing to lose! Everything to gain! Triumph beckons. You'll soon be feasting at richly spread tables and savouring the best comestibles, as lauded as Hayley. Dare you refuse?
BLAKE:	I shall have to consult with Cate –
HAYLEY:	Meditate on that door, which is ever open to Felpham's sweetling vale, wherein the hermit's constant patronage awaits.
	(HAYLEY *makes for the street door*.)
	And now he must catch a chaise to that village beyond compare, far from this wretched Pandemonium. A friend hopes you soon shall join him. Good day, good Blake.
BLAKE:	Many thanks sir.
HAYLEY:	Felpham is calling. You must hear it calling!
	(*Exit* HAYLEY.)
BLAKE:	Leave the Eternal City of my Visions? What kindness has London ever showed me? Years of neglect and all the time ever more ugly.
	Once was I could walk over Westminster Bridge straight to St. George's pleasant fields and

onwards to pretty villages but now increasingly stone all around.

The rural could always revive me. Success amongst the squirearchy? Hayley is an important man. A path to my epics' popular airing?

(*Enter* CATHERINE, *miserable*.)

What is it?

(CATHERINE *dumps her shopping down*.)

Come on – out with it. Your face is as long as the Bible.

(*Pause*.)

CATHERINE: There is a broken watering trough just beside the butchers. A crowd was gathered round something laid beside it. The body of a young man. A fellow who'd been kneeling rose. Haughty looking. Think he was a doctor. "Quite dead," he said, and I could see 'twas Robert on the cobbled ground. I shoved aside gawpers. "Hey!" they jostled but I fought me way through. Sank to my knees. Cradled his head. He'd brought up that broth I'd gave him. We didn't realise how bad he was.

BLAKE: Oh Lord...

CATHERINE: Then came a cart and they bunged him on. I told them his name and where he studied. Another one dead.

BLAKE: Gone into Eternity.

CATHERINE: I saw no spirit rising.

(*Pause*.)

BLAKE: Everyone I love dies.

CATHERINE: Everyone?

BLAKE: I need you, Milton. I need your words' consolation.

(BLAKE *sees* MILTON *appear, mourning.*)

MILTON: "We scarce in thousands meet one kindred mind,
And if the long-sought goal at last we find,
When least we fear it, death our treasure steals,
And gives our heart a wound which nothing heals."

BLAKE: How do I cope?

(MILTON *goes.*)

Milton? Milton!

CATHERINE: Another corpse for you to talk to instead of talking to me.

(BLAKE *turns back to his wife.*)

BLAKE: No one means more to me than you.

CATHERINE: They each do! Every dead poet. Every dead boy. Every dead book.

BLAKE: You mean all.

CATHERINE: Prove it.

BLAKE: How?

CATHERINE: Get me out of this hell!

(*Pause.*)

BLAKE: Cate, we have received an offer and we are accepting it. We're moving to where Mister Hayley will persistently employ me and make me the toast of the Sussex gentry.

CATHERINE: You're kidding.

BLAKE: There is a small, beautiful village by the name of Felpham…

CATHERINE: I feel alight just hearing the name.

BLAKE: We must prepare. Say our goodbyes to our friends. Leave this seat of woe London. We are departing.

CATHERINE: Departing!

BLAKE: (*Nods*) Departing.

The softest, most pleasing village. Far more spiritual that London. Heaven opes on every side. Windows unobstructed by vapours. Distinctly hearing celestial voices. Angel forms as clear as day. The most perfect little cottage in creation!

CATHERINE: I am sold.

(*The London light goes down on them and Felpham appears all beautiful.*)

SCENE TWO

(*The light of a country morning arises.* BLAKE *is alone in the small garden of Rose Cottage, Felpham. He yawns, rubs his eyes, stretches, and slaps himself round the face. He breathes deep then looks around the garden. He bends over a thistle.*)

BLAKE: Good morning, Mister Thistle! I don't feel very sharp today. How about you?

(*Thistle's voice.*)

"Oh, very sharp. I'm fairly bristling!"

(*A pretty country maid,* MARY, *enters.*)

MARY: Watch for the prick on him.

(BLAKE *looks up at her.*)

I always do.

BLAKE: I'll wager you do. A fair morn.

MARY: 'Tis a nice one.

BLAKE: Generous angels today.

MARY: Eh?

BLAKE: Shedding their sunlight.

MARY: I've had my eye on you.

BLAKE: Have you?

MARY: Been here about a year now ain't you?

BLAKE: A year and a half.

MARY: You're that big gentleman's servant ain't you?

BLAKE: I am in his employ.

MARY: He's an important gentleman. Always going up to London ain't he?

BLAKE: I came here from London.

MARY: What d'you wanna do that for?

BLAKE: London's... hectic.

MARY: I'd love to visit. Heard it's so big! Beautiful houses and palaces. Sights to gawp at. Important folk. Have to find a gentleman who'll take me.

BLAKE: Perhaps I'll take you.

MARY: (*Smirks*) You ain't no gentleman. You got a wife.

BLAKE: Very sharp-eyed.

MARY: Nowt else to do round here. 'Cept walk and eat and sleep.

BLAKE: And...?

MARY: You ain't no gentleman at all! I got to go to work. You get back to "Mister Thistle".

BLAKE: He's a little mean old man to me. I see this garden not with my eye corporeal but with inner visions, seeing thousands of neglected poems waiting to be picked up by a bard. Earthworms burrow in the dark damp soil. Spiders wait in their woven webs. Slugs leave slime in slow sullen wakes. Caterpillars feed on sweetest leaves. Butterflies burst forth from chrysalis sleep! Forms of the soul.

MARY: You tire my brain out.

BLAKE: What d'you work as?

MARY: Maid ain't I? To Lady Bathurst up at manor.

BLAKE: And what is the name of Bathurst's pretty maid?

MARY: Mary.

BLAKE: I'm William.

MARY: Ooh-er! I've met me a Willy.

BLAKE: Farewell for now, sweet Mary.

MARY: I'll see Willy later...

(*Exit MARY.*)

BLAKE: Your sins are all forgiven thee!

(*He walks from the garden into the cottage.* CATHERINE BLAKE *is in the kitchen singing as she prepares breakfast.*)

CATHERINE: "Little Tom is a cottager's son,
His years not amounting to ten!
But the dawn of his manhood begun
With a soul like the noblest of men."

BLAKE: Rather sing Hayley's verses now, would you?

CATHERINE: It's a nice poem. Where you been?

BLAKE: An early morning stroll.

CATHERINE: In bed after I've gone to sleep, up afore I'm awake. Might as well be a spinster. Eaten owt?

BLAKE: No.

CATHERINE: There's an egg on the stove.

BLAKE: An egg!

(BLAKE *goes to the egg, considers it.*)

Image of mundanity.

CATHERINE: It's going to be one of them mornings...

BLAKE: The unborn spirit trapped in the mundane shell. All enclosed in earth-bound rounds. Not seeing the sky, it will soar in after hatching.

CATHERINE: Should have done you oats.

(*He grabs a pencil and begins composing.*)

BLAKE: "To see the world in a grain of sand
And heaven in a wild flower
Hold infinity in the palm of your hand

	And eternity in an hour."
CATHERINE:	That's beautiful, Will.
	(CATHERINE *kisses* BLAKE's *hand*.)
	Want your egg hard boiled or soft?
BLAKE:	Least I get the odd lyric. The epic eludes. The day is devoured by other business. I use the night.
CATHERINE:	What time you come to bed?
BLAKE:	'Bout four.
CATHERINE:	And up afore seven? Tire yourself out.
BLAKE:	Just 'cos we're in paradise, the world don't cease. Still fields which should be crop-sown are turned to human sacrifice plots. Must not switch knowledge off though Felpham lull me. I came here to work.
CATHERINE:	Hard-boiled it'll have to be.
	(CATHERINE *takes the egg out of the pan and readies it to serve*.)
BLAKE:	I know my task. To tell the story of everything. 'Twas shown me. If I can't tell that tale my life means naught. An atom without true identity.
	(CATHERINE *serves him the egg*.)
CATHERINE:	Here you is.
BLAKE:	My vision shattered. Can't be put together again!
	(BLAKE *knocks the egg over and it shatters onto the floor*.)
	O! Stupid! Clumsy!
CATHERINE:	I'll cook you another one.
BLAKE:	I'm very hungry.
CATHERINE:	Your inspiration will return in time.

BLAKE: I never get time!

(*A knock on the door.* BLAKE *groans.* CATHERINE *goes to the door and opens it.* HAYLEY *walks in.*)

HAYLEY: Greetings to the splendid brace of Blakes!

CATHERINE: Morning, Mister Hayley. How are you?

HAYLEY: All the better for clapping me failing vision 'pon you.

(HAYLEY *kisses* CATHERINE's *hand.*)

And how is our enthusiastic seer?

CATHERINE: 'Bout to eat an egg.

HAYLEY: Delicious gift of the clucking clan.

CATHERINE: He's had one on the floor already.

HAYLEY: An egg smashed?

BLAKE: Knocked it off the table.

HAYLEY: What doth this Humpty mishap portend?

CATHERINE: He's in a bit of a grump.

HAYLEY: The egg was wrecked in a fit of spleen?!

CATHERINE: 'Twas an accident. He didn't get much sleep.

HAYLEY: Pray why not?

CATHERINE: He's worried.

HAYLEY: About?

CATHERINE: Fretting about the war.

HAYLEY: In a fidget over our Boney battles?

BLAKE: Even tucked in Felpham, some of us can't sleep.

HAYLEY: Still at your epic?

BLAKE: I am.

HAYLEY: Conscientious bard!

BLAKE:	Did you get a chance to look at the section I have you?
HAYLEY:	The hermit did. He noted they deal with warfare.
BLAKE:	My epic oft concerns Mankind's foolish battles.
HAYLEY:	Hayley will kindly share with you his educated opinion then will tell you of today's great historical news.
BLAKE:	Great historical news, sir?
HAYLEY:	Great historical news, sirrah, which might help to put your creative efforts into some perspective. But first let the bard impart his estimation. Your interesting voice does possess – this commentator admits – a kind of muscular brashness. But one fears that your lines will never do.
BLAKE:	Never do!?
HAYLEY:	Who desires such roughage?
BLAKE:	Some men love the truth.
HAYLEY:	The truth cannot be eat unsugared and also – this expert believes – so obscure.
BLAKE:	What could be clearer than...
CATHERINE:	Will! Let Mister Hayley explain.
BLAKE:	(*To* HAYLEY) Go on.
HAYLEY:	Lovers of poesy are gentle refined folk who yearn to nibble 'pon soft foodstuffs. This verse of yours is hard to chew and harder still to swallow.
BLAKE:	Is it?
HAYLEY:	'Tis.
BLAKE:	These so-refined folk – these poesy pathetics – do they deny war?

HAYLEY;	Which war?
BLAKE:	What?!
CATHERINE:	Will!
BLAKE:	Death reigns. Thousands of lives are bereft. Blackened the Sun which shines within us. The Universal Brotherhood denied destroyed downtrodden daily wasted.
HAYLEY:	Your hermit has not told you yet the momentous news. Historical news. Very important news.
BLAKE:	I think he better had tell.
HAYLEY:	Peace is declared.
BLAKE:	What?
HAYLEY:	The warring parties at Amiens have signed a treaty. The battle's defunct. Peace rules. All is well and so you see, your verses complaining 'gainst war become unnecessary.
CATHERINE:	Praise God and all his Saints!
BLAKE:	Can this be true?
HAYLEY:	As the evidence of senses.
BLAKE:	Is the morning come?
HAYLEY:	Dawn blazes.
CATHERINE:	Now we can settle down here and stop worrying.
BLAKE:	This puts a different complexion...
HAYLEY:	You may away tuck your difficult and indigestible stanzas and concentrate 'pon those talents which might tempt dame Fortune your way. Mister Blake, your caring patron has ideas unto your future path which you shall concur are extempore. The hermit proposes a marriage betwixt his lines and your engraver. He has been busy composing verses

	upon a subject palatable – "Ballads Based upon Anecdotes Relating to Animals". Interesting odes to valiant pets and vicious untamed things. These trinkets you shall illustrate. They will be sold as broadsheets and the profits be all thine.
CATHERINE:	Mister Hayley, you are too generous. Ain't it a stunning idea, Will?
BLAKE:	Staggering.
HAYLEY:	The months ahead will see you pupping a dog, in labour with a lion, tossing off an elephant.
BLAKE:	Elevated tasks.
HAYLEY:	The inaugural ballad tells the tale of a pretty cur named Fido who sacrifices his life to save his master from a ravening croc.
CATHERINE:	Is this not brilliant, Mister Blake?
BLAKE:	I am speechless at the prospect.
HAYLEY:	'Tis only one of many promising projects your patron has in mind for you, that Fortune might catch you in her snare. You are a man of brush as well as engraver?
BLAKE:	I am.
HAYLEY:	Fame as a portrait painter awaits you!
BLAKE:	A portrait painter?!
HAYLEY:	Society esteems its own visage. Why this very afternoon you will meet the hermit's interesting friend, the important Lady Bathurst. One of our biggest local nobs.
BLAKE:	Must be an extraordinary woman.

HAYLEY:	She has heard all a propos the enthusiastic London artist residing in Felpham. She has expressed great interest in seeing him.
CATHERINE:	Oh, Mister Hayley sir! William, give our best friend ever a thousand million thanks.
BLAKE:	Here's one at least. Thank you, Mister Hayley.
HAYLEY:	What say you to these schemes?
BLAKE:	Suddenly everything's happening so fast. I was beginning to think that Felpham provided as little luck as London.
HAYLEY:	Hard times are over. War is finished. Success beckons. Blake shall be the name on all society's best lips. Meet the hermit at his turret at half an hour post ten o'the clock and we shall ride together to Lady Bathurst, to whom you shall bow and gently woo. Until then fond thoughts from a loving patron.
BLAKE:	My gratitude forever.
CATHERINE:	You are our saviour.
HAYLEY:	The hermit acts from his heart's promptings. Be there at the appointed hour.
BLAKE:	Will do.
HAYLEY:	Good morning, thou fair Blake-ess.
CATHERINE:	Thanks ever so much.
HAYLEY:	Try not to break another egg! (*Exit* HAYLEY, *chuckling*.)
BLAKE:	An egg now seems most attractive.
CATHERINE:	Your wish is my command.

BLAKE: If that crew of political ruffians can reach a peace agreement, then hope is four-hundred-fold increased. Albion begins a culture of brotherhood.

CATHERINE: Must grab at these possibilities.

BLAKE: The main chance back. I had thought it long gone.

CATHERINE: Money to be made.

BLAKE: Wonder what Bathurst's like?

CATHERINE: Now you behave.

BLAKE: Resentment is vanishing. Futurity shines bright. I'll woo the world anew. First, I'll tuck into this delightful eggy.

CATHERINE: Might be able to afford a new dress...

(T*he* BLAKES *fade into the calm of a Felpham morning.*)

SCENE THREE

(*The sitting room of* LADY BATHURST's *manor house appears in a gloomy light.* LADY BATHURST, *old and decrepit, sits amongst her expensive furnishings and collection of old paintings, each showing views of nature and crumbling masonry.* MARY, *in maidservant's garb, enters.*)

BATHURST: (*Muttering*) Where is she? Where is she?

MARY: You rang, ma'am?

BATHURST: 'Twas so long ago, I had almost forgot.

MARY: Sorry for any delay, ma'am.

(*Pause.*)

What were it you wanted, ma'am?

BATHURST: You see how tedious postponement is, yes? I've a good mind to keep you on tenterhooks there for three hours. I could, you know. Keep you standing there without even leave to urinate.

MARY: I am at her Ladyship's command.

BATHURST: That is the fact of it! I called you here to bring to your attention something which irritates. Do you see yonder representation of the wrecked and aged folly?

MARY: This painting of a clapped-out old ruin, ma'am?

BATHURST: Hush! 'Tis a tower has been struck by lightning. Do you notice my vexation?

MARY: No ma'am.

BATHURST: 'Tis all of a wonk! Can you conceive how much that grates me? Sat here all day, perusing my collection, savouring my favourite semblance, finding it off-kilter! 'Tis a torture of hell, miss. Set it right.

MARY:	No sooner said as done.
	(*MARY corrects the picture.*)
	Can I ask you something, ma'am?
BATHURST:	Ignorance learns by quizzing its betters.
MARY:	Why d'you like 'em so much?
BATHURST:	What?
MARY:	Pictures of buildings all falling down and that.
BATHURST:	The reason is… Do you dare to question my taste, minx?
MARY:	Oh no ma'am.
BATHURST:	I have a connoisseur's eye. The likes of you can never comprehend. Another little task now if it is not too much trouble. My feet are of an ache. Fetch me my foot-spa.
MARY:	Of course, ma'am.
BATHURST:	Lukewarm water and a drop of Daisy's milk.
MARY:	Yes ma'am.
BATHURST:	Sometime today.
MARY:	Ma'am.
	(*Exit* MARY.)
BATHURST:	Ignorant bitch.
	(*Slight pause.*)
	O where is that footbath? Wretch has been gone three hours!
	(BATHURST *glowers. Enter* MARY.)
	Is it ready yet?
MARY:	Oh no ma'am. I haven't had time…
BATHURST:	Why this reappearance?

MARY:	Mister Hayley is here ma'am.
BATHURST:	Hayley? Here? Why? Oh Why?!
MARY:	Says you're expecting him.
BATHURST:	Is he a foetus?
MARY:	I don't under...
BATHURST:	Will you keep your superiors waiting? Show him in!
MARY:	Ma'am!

(*Exit* MARY.)

BATHURST:	This nincompoop! Did ever a damned soul suffer as I?

(*Enter* MARY *with* HAYLEY.)

MARY:	Mister Hayley ma'am.

(HAYLEY *steps forward*.)

HAYLEY:	Fairest belle of Sussex fields, salutations from a bending hermit who has sneaked beyond his lonely cell to homage a beauty both rarefied and refined.
BATHURST:	Thank you Mary, that will be all.
MARY:	Ma'am.

(*Exit* MARY.)

BATHURST:	Hayley looms again, does he?
HAYLEY:	He cannot keep long at a distance.
BATHURST:	So, it seems. Do sit down, sir.
HAYLEY:	Where do you wish your hermit's fond rump?
BATHURST:	Over there I would deem a suitably pleasant distance.

(BATHURST *points to a seat some way from her.*)

HAYLEY: Indeed 'tis.

(HAYLEY *sits where instructed*.)

BATHURST: What brings the man Hayley to my manor this morn? So soon after his previous haunting.

HAYLEY: Has the good old lady lost her faculties? Is her memory a goose?

BATHURST: Is this impudence?

HAYLEY: I but jest. Do not you recall, beauty, that today your loyal scout after talent did vow to fetch you a promising specimen of the species of painter engraver.

BATHURST: I do not remember.

HAYLEY: Does the name Blake not ring any bells?

BATHURST: Not for me.

HAYLEY: But your fishing friend told you – did he not? – of his latest catch. Newly moved from London and now at the hermit's side. Here this morn for your inspection.

BATHURST: A blessed bore! But if the rendezvous was prior arranged...

HAYLEY: Your servant assures that it will be worth your while, beauty.

BATHURST: And I tell Hayley that it will take a special example of man indeed to pique my interest today.

HAYLEY: Dear madam, Blake is an original.

(HAYLEY *rises*.)

BATHURST: I saw once a ballet-dancing ape described thus. I did enjoy her.

HAYLEY: Ha ha ha!

(*Exit* HAYLEY.)

BATHURST: She was better looking than you, my hermit.

(BATHURST *laughs then coughs, nearly chokes. Enter* HAYLEY *with* BLAKE. BATHURST *surveys them.*)

HAYLEY: Lady Bathurst, the hermit proudly introduces to you William Blake, enthusiastic practitioner of the engraver's stippling art.

BLAKE: (*Aside*) Never stippling!

HAYLEY: Mister Blake – Lady Bathurst.

BLAKE: How do ye do?

BATHURST: How do I do what?

HAYLEY: The suppliant was asking on your well-being.

BATHURST: What's he want – a place in my will?

HAYLEY: (*To* BLAKE) Her Ladyship loves chortling.

BLAKE: I see.

HAYLEY: (*To* BATHURST) May we sit down?

BATHURST: Pray do. My neck begins to crick.

(*Aside*) Damn looking up at lessers!

(HAYLEY *motions for* BLAKE *to sit.* BLAKE *sits rather close to* BATHURST, *who baulks.*)

Unfortunate proximity!

(HAYLEY *takes his previous position.*)

HAYLEY: Waning goddess, Mister Blake is now resident in Felpham and is employed as amanuensis to Cowper's hard-working biographer.

BLAKE: (*Aside*) Amanuensis!

BATHURST: Really?

HAYLEY:	He is working on the plates for that "Life" on which all society waits, breath baited.
BATHURST:	Cowper was a piquant loon. Has his memoirist discovered much gossip of his existence?
HAYLEY:	The hermit's 'Life of Cowper' will he hopes be above trivia, ma'am.
BATHURST:	I fear society shall reject it.
HAYLEY:	Mister Blake is soon to impart upon an interesting representation of the genius's tame hares.
BATHURST:	Cowper kept tame hares?
HAYLEY:	He did.
BATHURST:	That is fascinating. I would love to retain badgers myself, but I fear my groundsman would bate them.
BLAKE:	He is a master bater then?
	(BLAKE *laughs. The others look at him in silence.*)
	Country folk often are...
HAYLEY:	Aside from working on engravings for that "Cowper", Mister Blake has other jobs in hand. He is to illustrate some "Ballads" by the hermit. They shall be released as monthly broadsheets. Perhaps the lady might subscribe?
BATHURST:	Shall consider it. Mister Blake, Sir Hayley provides you with plentiful work?
BLAKE:	I am eternally grateful.
HAYLEY:	"Laden up the donkey". But alas, for an enthusiast, no amount of work is enough. Mister Blake has a sweet, gentle wife to support. He is always on the look-out for commissions, and he is about to put upon his bow a gaudy new string.

BATHURST:	Which is?
HAYLEY:	He means to turn portrait painter. Is that not right, Mister Blake?
BLAKE:	I do fervently wish to paint portraits.
BATHURST:	I have never approved of sitting for portraits. Brings on the aching back. The aching head. The aching nether –
HAYLEY:	Belle!
BATHURST:	All for hideous slander removed from reality. Sir Joshua Reynolds painted me when I was a miss. Made me look heinous.
BLAKE:	Reynolds is the worst.
BATHURST:	Rot! I sold that painting for four hundred pounds. Impudence on the good Sir Josh.

(*She tuts.*)

HAYLEY:	Mister Blake forthright opines.
BATHURST:	Mister Blake can jump in the sea!
HAYLEY:	Faded lovely, please do not take offence at a city dolt, though he bring gutter manners into manors. The Blake meant no offence, did he?
BLAKE:	None at all!
HAYLEY:	Good Blake is excitable today. He is ecstatic at news from London.
BATHURST:	He is?
HAYLEY:	Are you not, good Blake?
BLAKE:	Thrilled and much relieved.
BATHURST:	I should not have thought that you had been familiar with Lady Sedgewick, let alone been elated at her inheritance.

BLAKE:	Lady Sedgewick's inheritance?!
BATHURST:	London's big news.
BLAKE:	I could not give a…
HAYLEY:	No! What Blake is fond of is war's decease.
BATHURST:	What fluff.
BLAKE:	We are beginning a New Age of Brotherhood.
BATHURST:	We have allowed the Frenchies too much.
BLAKE:	To stop death?
BATHURST:	From that libertine nation came forth Jacobinism. Swine feeding off their betters' severed heads.
BLAKE:	The terror was a result of our assisting the counterrevolutionaries. Had we supported the new government…
BATHURST:	Words smacking of sedition.
HAYLEY:	Mister Blake is a lover of fairness and all men.
BATHURST:	Only sluts and blind sodomites love all men. Carry on with such treason, sirrah, and you'll find a noose for a neckerchief.
	(BATHURST *glares at* BLAKE, *who squirms*.)
HAYLEY:	Mister Blake loves Sussex and especially Felpham. Lady B also loves these environs. The picturesque is a passion common to both of you.
BATHURST:	I love a pretty view. Do you?
BLAKE:	I do.
BATHURST:	Have you seen the sights hereabouts?
BLAKE:	Many of them. Why, the other night I glimpsed an unusual one.
BATHURST:	I doubt I've not seen it afore you.
BLAKE:	Did you ever see a faerie's funeral madam?

BATHURST:	Never, sir.
BLAKE:	I did the other night. I was walking alone when a great stillness descended upon the branches and flowers and a more than common softness hung in the air. I heard a low and pleasant sound, and I knew not from whence it came. At last, I saw the broad leaf of a flower move and underneath I saw a procession of creatures the size and colour of green grasshoppers bearing a body laid out on a rose leaf which they proceeded to bury with songs and then they all disappeared. It was a faerie funeral.
BATHURST:	Where did you see this freak, Mister Blake?
BLAKE:	In my own mind.
BATHURST:	I find myself of a sudden chilled, Mister Hayley! Methinks it would be better if you immediately took your fantastical friend away with you. I would not wish you to catch your death.
HAYLEY:	Lady Bathurst's concern is very kind. Blake, join the hermit in evacuating.
BLAKE:	Of course, sir.
HAYLEY:	Agéd and regal beauty, thanks for your hospitality. Perhaps you will keep the Blake in your thoughts?
BATHURST:	It shall be difficult to forget him.
HAYLEY:	If you could find him a job, he would be industrious and grateful.
BATHURST:	I'll think on't.
HAYLEY:	Farewell then. Good Blake, bid a lady fond adieu.
BLAKE:	God bless you dear Lady Bathurst.
BATHURST:	Goodbye, Master Blake.

HAYLEY:	(*To* BLAKE) The hermit shall join you in a moment. (*Exit* BLAKE. HAYLEY *turns to* BATHURST.) Parting is such sweet sorrow.
BATHURST:	It is sweet. Fine hermit Hayley, I have one request of you.
HAYLEY:	Grand dame, what is't?
BATHURST:	If I agree to set this Blake a task, promise me one thing.
HAYLEY:	Anything, enchantress.
BATHURST:	Never bring him near me again!
HAYLEY:	If that's beauty's wish.
BATHURST:	'Tis.
HAYLEY:	What little task will you set Blake? He cannot paint your portrait if you'll not see him.
BATHURST:	I require a new set of decorated screens. He can paint them. A country view incorporating some piece of fallen masonry would be acceptable. Six guineas.
HAYLEY:	The ancient ravisher is generous as always. (*Enter* MARY.)
BATHURST:	Ah, at last. Mister Hayley is leaving. Has his companion left the premises?
MARY:	He's waiting on the porch for Mister Hayley, ma'am.
BATHURST:	Hayley, a gentle riddance.
HAYLEY:	Same to you.
BATHURST:	Fare thee well.
	(HAYLEY *bows and goes.* BATHURST *barks at* MARY.)

	See that the door is locked and bolted after those gentlemen.
MARY:	Yes ma'am.
BATHURST:	Dastards in this house!
MARY:	Ma'am?
BATHURST:	A whiff of the stench of sedition. You, miss! Where is my foot-spa?
MARY:	I'll bring it you straight.
BATHURST:	Caught in an eternal wait!

(MARY *bobs and bows to* BATHURST *and rushes out the room in which all light fades.*)

SCENE FOUR

(*Evening time,* BLAKE *lights a candle in Rose cottage.* CATHERINE *sits shivering.*)

BLAKE: It is my belief that every picture hung upon a person's wall is their mirror. She's an old structure fallen to a decrepit state. She's civilisation in decadent decay. She is Mystery. Mother of abominations. Queen of harlots. Babylon!

CATHERINE: She can't be that bad.

BLAKE: I'm refusing the job.

CATHERINE: Now wait a minute…

BLAKE: I have never before turned down work…

CATHERINE: Six guineas!

BLAKE: It's a chore too far! Screens for a hag to change her stays behind.

CATHERINE: This is pride.

BLAKE: Ha!

CATHERINE: You're proud as Pharaoh. What are we sat here at?

BLAKE: Letting our dinner get down us.

CATHERINE: We're sat shivering!

BLAKE: It is peevish cold.

CATHERINE: This is spring! Our heavenly cottage is an icebox when foul weather hits. Hayley don't pay us enough for ample coal.

BLAKE: We do adequate, don't we?

CATHERINE: Mister Blake, you know I believe in you. But I don't think I can go through another winter like last. Agues and rheumatism.

BLAKE:	There's nothing I like less than seeing you suffer.
CATHERINE:	You're spoiling your chances, that's all.
BLAKE:	Catherine, don't become a wheel on which I am tortured for having failed you.
CATHERINE:	Paint her screens.
BLAKE:	I can't.
CATHERINE:	You won't.
BLAKE:	I won't!
CATHERINE:	Then maybe I won't be your wife.
BLAKE:	(*Rising*) I need air.
CATHERINE:	Off to the alehouse?
BLAKE:	So, what?
CATHERINE:	Can you afford it?
BLAKE:	I've enough for a jug of porter.

(BLAKE *makes for the door*.)

CATHERINE: If you paint her screens, you could afford jug after jug.

(*Exit* BLAKE.)

Bloody cold. In a room not much warmer than this, we sat and first spoke, years ago. You told me of your love-crosses, and I pitied you in my heart. "I love you for that!" you cried, and we began a-courting. Never imagined it'd become me shivering in a colder room on my own.

(CATHERINE *slumps in her chair as the cottage fades into gloom*.)

SCENE FIVE

(*An alehouse appears in the evening light.* BLAKE *enters with a jug and sits at a table.*)

BLAKE: Can't even get a decent glass of porter here. Must make do with scrumpy.

(*He sips.*)

Urgh. Made from the same crabby apples God forbade Adam. Who's here?

(*He peers round the pub.*)

Felpham folk. Cheery enough but I fear not companions for spiritual discourse nor discussing the problems of the prophetic life.

(*Enter* JOHN MILTON, *stony-faced as ever.*)

MILTON: What dost thou here, William?

BLAKE: I thirsted for the solace of strong liquor.

MILTON: As always, I remain sober.

BLAKE: Don't blame me for that. Get something down you!

(MILTON *turns his nose up.*)

They must have rare alehouses in Paradise.

MILTON: Frivolous prattle.

BLAKE: Notorious winebibber was Jesus.

(MILTON *is very disapproving.*)

Oh, come off your pulpit, man! Give me some cheer. God knows I need it.

MILTON: Thou art miserable?

BLAKE: A tortured soul. I've just had a row with the wife.

MILTON: Poor wretch! My first spouse and I were incompatibility's paradigm. Curse the Cupid who brought us together.

BLAKE: One can never trust those Greek gods. You never had a deal of luck with women, did you?

MILTON: The only dame along-side whom I discovered a state paradisiacal died but two years post the wedding night.

BLAKE: Life's a bitch, ain't it, John?

MILTON: My life was too many bitches.

(BLAKE *is surprised, then roars with laughter.*)

BLAKE: A joke quenches sorrow more than a sermon. Cate and I have this evening had the most useless row.

MILTON: Then might I interest you in a small, persuasively argued, and in its time popular pamphlet containing my animadversions respecting marital quandaries? Here.

(MILTON *hands* BLAKE *a pamphlet.*)

BLAKE: "The Doctrine and Discipline of Divorce."

MILTON: There are two sequels, should your interest be pricked.

BLAKE: So traditional about some things. So radical about others. You are a compound of contraries.

MILTON: My mind loves wrestling with problems. Females always were a problem for me.

BLAKE: Is it true that you forced your daughters to read to you in languages they didn't have?

MILTON: One tongue is enough for any girl.

(BLAKE *laughs, a bit scandalised.* MILTON *is smug that his humour is appreciated.*)

BLAKE:	I love Cate. I thought she comprehended. I've accepted many of her wishes. If it was up to me, I would often...
MILTON:	What?
	(*Enter* MARY *with a large bottle.* BLAKE *rises.*)
BLAKE:	Well met, Mary!
MARY:	Master Willy, you're here!
BLAKE:	Called in for a sup.
MARY:	Picking up ma's gin. Poor thing can't sleep without it.
MILTON:	Might I be introduced?
BLAKE:	Not now.
MARY:	Oh, why? Are you busy?
BLAKE:	Not at all.
MILTON:	Am I nothing at all?!
BLAKE:	Would you let me walk you home?
MARY:	Alright.
BLAKE:	Allow me.
	(BLAKE *takes the bottle from* MARY.)
MILTON:	I thought you had craved philosophical discourse, prophet to prophet.
BLAKE:	I said –
MARY:	What?
MILTON:	Plus a moan about the wife.
BLAKE:	Not now!
MARY:	Thought you meant now?
BLAKE:	I do!

MILTON: It seems thou art only in search of a ready and easy shag.
BLAKE: Ever the puritan.
MARY: You coming?
BLAKE: Mary, lead the way.

(MARY *and* BLAKE *exit as* MILTON *fades away*.)

SCENE SIX

(*In the dim candlelight of the cottage,* CATHERINE *shivers as she gets into bed alone. Darkness as she blows the candle out.*

The moon appears high in the night sky. And sheds its reflected light upon BLAKE *and* MARY *in a barn, post-coital.*)

MARY:	You didn't mind doing it in a barn?
BLAKE:	It was good enough for Jesus to be born in…
MARY:	(*Laughs*) You'll get us struck dead by God, you will.
BLAKE:	He's not such a tyrant as that.
MARY:	Know him, do you?
BLAKE:	He and I are acquainted.
MARY:	You are a queer one. I like here nights. Quiet. Can do owt you like.
BLAKE:	The window lets in the moonlight. Reflected glory. Alright for night hours, nothing wrong with it.
MARY:	I scarce understand a word you say.
BLAKE:	Sorry.
MARY:	Everyone thinks you're odd. Some people don't like you for it.
BLAKE:	It has ever been that way. Who?
MARY:	My mistress for one.
BLAKE:	I don't like her!
MARY:	Don't speak ill of your betters.
BLAKE:	She's not my better.
MARY:	She has more money than you.
BLAKE:	I don't care a fig about that.
MARY:	Then why you sniffing round her for work?

BLAKE: I must eat.

MARY: Exactly.

BLAKE: Don't you think it would be healthier if we weren't dependent on the likes of her?

MARY: My mistress knows you think like that. I hear her staggering down the hall, cursing that you ought to be hung.

BLAKE: She wants to kill me?!

MARY: She's barmy. Just stop your "down the rich" talk and you'll be fine. You're nice. We gonna meet again?

BLAKE: I don't like lying to my wife.

MARY: You are odd.

BLAKE: I shall tell her about you. That I am taking a second love. It was good enough for Abraham...

MARY: She'll pull my hair out!

BLAKE: She must transcend her jealousy.

MARY: (*Weeping*) I'll lose me job if I'm thought an whore.

BLAKE: I won't tell her about you.

MARY: Promise?

BLAKE: I promise.

(MARY *stops crying*.)

MARY: Still like to see you again.

BLAKE: Don't you long for another world?

MARY: Never thought 'bout it.

BLAKE: The moon is sad. Wishes she didn't have to rely on another for light.

MARY: Gotta go.

BLAKE:	Now?
MARY:	Ma worries.
BLAKE:	I'll see you around.
MARY:	Okey-doke.
	(MARY *goes.* BLAKE *sits staring at the moon. Enter* MILTON.)
BLAKE:	Come to lay me out on a rack of guilt?
MILTON:	'Tis but a transient injury. To be forgiven once and again. Get back to your wife.
BLAKE:	You and your God are perhaps not so harsh after all.
MILTON:	The greater offence is spiritual adultery.
BLAKE:	What's that?
MILTON:	Betraying vision. Selling your soul. Wearing Satan's livery. Working for the adversary. Then thou art truly damned.
BLAKE:	You're saying that's what I'm at?
MILTON:	Cap fits, wear it.
	(MILTON *vanishes.*)
BLAKE:	Lots of times lately I've been feeling sad and empty. I meet a pretty girl. Find a faerie. Walk on the beach. Commune with nature 'til my heart's content. But my epic goes unwritten. Which blight infects all moments of attraction and communion. Have I forgot this earth's not yet a paradise for all?
	(*A cloud passes over the moon, enveloping* BLAKE *in darkness.*)

ACT TWO

SCENE SEVEN

(*The cold light of day hits* CATHERINE BLAKE *in the cottage. She is colouring in a manuscript of* BLAKE's. *A knock at the door.* CATHERINE *answers it.* HAYLEY *stands there.*)

HAYLEY: The fair Blake-ess! A pleasant morning to you.

CATHERINE: Do come in, sir.

(HAYLEY *enters.*)

HAYLEY: Hayley is always delighted by entering your snug hovel.

CATHERINE: Mister Blake has gone to Chichester to buy inks.

HAYLEY: It is upon you the hermit comes a-calling. He has a present for you. A copy of his "Triumphs of Temper".

(HAYLEY *gives* CATHERINE *the book.*)

CATHERINE: Thank you very much, sir.

HAYLEY: That edition has in it your husband's engravings. Embellishing Hayley brings out his best.

(HAYLEY *has wandered to the worktable.*)

He left amid work?

CATHERINE: I am colouring this.

HAYLEY: You?!

CATHERINE: He hasn't time for everything. Mister Flaxman put a fellow onto us wants a copy of the songs.

HAYLEY: Such a wife! How lucky the Blake do be.

CATHERINE: Try telling him that.

HAYLEY:	Surely, he must be gratefully aware. He ought to have been lumbered with the hermit's spouse. Poor, flighty, splenetic, frigid Eliza! In life she was the bane of her husband's existence. In death she left him sad and alone. William is blessed with your company.
CATHERINE:	Remind him of that, would you?

(CATHERINE *is suddenly seized by a coughing fit.*)

HAYLEY:	Why heavens! Mrs Blake, what is the matter?
CATHERINE:	'Tis nothing. Twill pass.
HAYLEY:	Let a concerned hermit fetch water.
CATHERINE:	Don't trouble. Oh!

(CATHERINE *coughs violently.* HAYLEY *fetches a cup of water for her. She takes and drinks it.*)

	That's better.
HAYLEY:	My fair lady is ill?
CATHERINE:	I am.
HAYLEY:	Commiserations.
CATHERINE:	I get agues and rheumatism.
HAYLEY:	Why cause these punishments of Egypt, fair ma'am?
CATHERINE:	Look around. You can't miss the reason.
HAYLEY:	Hayley cannot guess...
CATHERINE:	This place.
HAYLEY:	Oh.
CATHERINE:	This cold, draughty, mildewed place of damp and rattling windows. It's doing its best to kill me.
HAYLEY:	Why don't you move?
CATHERINE:	How can we afford to?

HAYLEY: Have you not enough money coming in?

CATHERINE: We have not.

HAYLEY: Then is your patron faced with a mystery. Why does your husband turn work down?

CATHERINE: Indeed.

HAYLEY: His first duty should be to care for you.

CATHERINE: That's far from being a priority. He turns down jobs because he's too proud. He cares very little about me. Do you know...? No, I cannot tell.

HAYLEY: The hermit offers caring ears.

CATHERINE: If Mister Blake cared for me, would he suggest a second wife?

HAYLEY: What?!

CATHERINE: That's what he suggests.

HAYLEY: Mrs Blake, you know Hayley loves your husband with a father's love. Sometimes fathers must speak out! Your husband has folly-filled notions. He will end up destitute and perfectly mad. He must cease challenging decent standards. He'll be flung outside of society. He'll drag you with him. Imagine that!

CATHERINE: Oh, I do!

HAYLEY: Do you wish your loving patron to have a word with him?

CATHERINE: I don't know.

HAYLEY: We two must work together at this.

CATHERINE: If you think it'll help.

(HAYLEY takes CATHERINE's *hand*.)

HAYLEY:	If you were wed to the hermit, you would not find yourself thus neglected.
	(*Enter* BLAKE *muttering to himself.*)
BLAKE:	I have been gullible...
	(*He notices* HAYLEY *paying court to his wife.*)
HAYLEY:	Ah, the Blake! Returned from a Chichester trip?
BLAKE:	You did not expect me so soon?
CATHERINE:	You get the inks?
BLAKE:	Yes, and I get the gist of this.
	(*To* HAYLEY) Sir, you believe it is time for a change?
HAYLEY:	What, pray, import you?
BLAKE:	Fed up with no wife of your own?
HAYLEY:	Hold on, sir.
BLAKE:	It seems that, after all, I have something you have not.
HAYLEY:	Gentle Blake!
CATHERINE:	(*To* BLAKE) Are you jealous, William?
BLAKE:	Take her! You've had everything else.
HAYLEY:	What?!
BLAKE:	I see who thou art.
HAYLEY:	Your friend and ever-loving patron.
BLAKE:	Get behind me.
HAYLEY:	What the...?
BLAKE:	Thou art Satan!
HAYLEY:	The hermit dare not think there's a need for this!
BLAKE:	I see your wiles.
	(*To* CATHERINE) He's been proposing, I suppose, that I give up my mad ways?

CATHERINE: You always were intuitive.

BLAKE: My nose for bullshit...

HAYLEY: Sirrah!

BLAKE: Is this morning extra-long. When I arrived in Chichester, you know what I saw?

HAYLEY: Something which put you in a detestable mood.

BLAKE: Too right. They're drafting in dragoons in case the French invade. The war's back!

CATHERINE: No!

BLAKE: An ignorant fool was I. I should have known that Satan's peace was but a pause for rearmament. I've been asleep on Delilah's lap. Oh, here's a Philistine with his shears!

HAYLEY: Dreadful news.

BLAKE: You love war! You'd have me the lapdog to its perpetrators.

HAYLEY: I fear this begins to smack of spleen.

BLAKE: Not spleen, sir. Anger. I am sick of skulking here.

HAYLEY: Oh, are you?

BLAKE: At your beck and call.

CATHERINE: Will...

BLAKE: Thou affected hermit-crab! If you wish me to continue in your employ, you'll stump up more money. The only reason I even entertain working for you...

CATHERINE: Here we go.

BLAKE: Is to pay for my own schemes. But your pittance isn't enough.

HAYLEY: What is this the hermit smells?

BLAKE:	I am heartily sick of that! "The hermit. Hayley. Your patron." Why can't you refer to yourself as "I" like the poor bloody rest of us!
HAYLEY:	(*Spluttering*) But... The hermit... Mrs Blake!
CATHERINE:	Your habit is irritating.
HAYLEY:	Very well then, madam, and sir. I say what I smell. Ungratefulness. Monstrous ingratitude! 'Tis enough to make a soul turn Timon. After all I have done for you.
BLAKE:	What have you done? Pestered and badgered me with fool schemes. I made a loss on the "Ballads"!
HAYLEY:	In that case, I'll pester you no more. Good day, rancorous Blakes.
BLAKE:	Good day to you.
HAYLEY:	I will say this: you'd better watch it. Your ways are not popular. You'll find yourself a bundle of trouble.
BLAKE:	Is that a threat?
HAYLEY:	I merely observe.
BLAKE:	Not so loving now!
HAYLEY:	Fare thee well.
	(*Exit* HAYLEY. *The* BLAKES *eye each other.*)
CATHERINE:	Now you've done it.
BLAKE:	I do believe I have. I feel stifled. I'll sit in the garden. Join me?
CATHERINE:	In a little.
BLAKE:	Don't be too long.
	(BLAKE *leaves for the garden.* CATHERINE *sits and coughs. The light fades on her.*)

SCENE EIGHT

(*Daylight shines upon* BLAKE *in the garden on Rose Cottage. He mutters darkly to himself.*)

BLAKE: War again! Killing again! And I illustrate ballads to nincompoop animals! My birth right is sold for a mess of pottage. I shall be reprimanded.

(*A drunken soldier,* SKOLFIELD, *appears.*)

SKOLFIELD: First sign of Bedlam, that. Talking to thyself.

BLAKE: I beg your pardon?

SKOLFIELD: Why, didst thou fart?

(SKOLFIELD *blows a raspberry, laughs.*)

Thought there was a pong.

BLAKE: Why are you in my garden?

SKOLFIELD: "My garden"! I wants a word with thee.

BLAKE: You may have a word – farewell!

SKOLFIELD: Why, where you going?

BLAKE: On the contrary, it is you are going.

SKOLFIELD: On the cuntery? Disgusting! I need a piss.

BLAKE: Piss off.

SKOLFIELD: You'll not speak like that at me! Have you seen what I'm wearing?

BLAKE: Shame's garb.

SKOLFIELD: You what?

BLAKE: The attire of cannon fodder.

SKOLFIELD: It is the King's land I protect!

BLAKE: Get out.

SKOLFIELD: Oi now!

(*Enter* CATHERINE.)

CATHERINE: What's all this shouting in aid of?
BLAKE: (*Pointing to* SKOLFIELD) That.
CATHERINE: What's it want?
SKOLFIELD: Oi!
BLAKE: It wants some manners teaching.
SKOLFIELD: Who's this, your mother?
CATHERINE: Bloody cheek!
SKOLFIELD: Watch your French! Old trout.
CATHERINE: Get it out of here, William.
BLAKE: I am attempting to remove it.
SKOLFIELD: You insult the people of England!
BLAKE: England's people? A parcel of fools.
SKOLFIELD: What you say?!
BLAKE: Letting themselves be dragged in another war. They play with fire, they'll get burned!
SKOLFIELD: I'll remember you said that.
BLAKE: You'll report me?
SKOLFIELD: I will!
BLAKE: I begin to see. Then hear this: the people of England are slaves to the King!
SKOLFIELD: Oh, gawd blimey!
BLAKE: He'll draw them to squalid deaths.
CATHERINE: He'll pull us into a fire and none of us might get out.
SKOLFIELD: Oh, my lord!

BLAKE:	I know that you've been sent here to spy by Esquire Hayley. Damn him. Damn you. And damn the King!
SKOLFIELD:	Damn the King?!
BLAKE:	Damn all Kings to hell! All soldiers are slaves.
CATHERINE:	Get off out of here!
BLAKE:	Out you go!

(BLAKE *grabs* SKOLFIELD *and pushes him out.*)

Ignorant ape!

SKOLFIELD:	Watch who you're pushing!
BLAKE:	Damn the King!
SKOLFIELD:	Treason!
BLAKE:	Out of my garden!
SKOLFIELD:	Watch it!
BLAKE:	Damn the King!!!

(BLAKE *shoves* SKOLFIELD *out and up the road.*)

CATHERINE: That's it! Box his ears. Get him out! That's it! That's the spirit! That is the spirit...

(*She sags.*)

...that soon deflates.

(*The sky darkens.*)

All of a shake.

(*Re-enter BLAKE.*)

BLAKE:	I pushed him to The Fox, him shouting all the way there. He accused me of treason.
CATHERINE:	I feel sick.
BLAKE:	I too feel nervous fear. Traitor's hang. Is this the bundle of trouble Hayley threatened me with?

(BLAKE *and* CATHERINE *look at each other in trepidation as clouds overwhelm the sky.*)

SCENE NINE

(*In a darkened room,* SKOLFIELD *is giving a deposition.*)

SKOLFIELD: I'm an Englishman and ought to be treated right. An. English. Man. Me old Dad taught me to be a man. Learnt me that lesson so I'll never forget.

(*Mimes a thrashing.*)

"YOU ARE A DISGRACE TO ME! ACT LIKE A MAN DOES, YOU LITTLE SWINE!"

(*Calms.*)

I learnt. I become a man. Always done man's work. Lifting, carrying, building. Fighting! Army taught me to be English. Learnt me that lesson so I'll never forget.

(*Mimes a flogging.*)

"YOU ARE A DISGRACE TO THE ARMY! ACT LIKE A SOLDIER, YOU HORRIBLE SWINE!"

(*Calms.*)

I learnt. I am a soldier. I been on battlefields. Mates fallin' round me. Bits of them showering. Knee deep in blood. This Blake bloke has no respect. Rude as soon as he sees me. It's like the sight of me uniform enraged him. Then it all comes out.

(SKOLFIELD *leans forward.*)

He said that the people of England are a parcel of children what ought to get scalded. He said that Bonaparte should become master of all. He said Frenchie should cut our throats. Then he... I can hardly bring myself to say it! He damned the King. He did! Damned him! Damned his country too.

Damned his subjects. Said us soldiers are the King's slaves, and he damned all the bloody poor people to boot. Then she showed up. His wife. She says, "the King can run into a fire and not come out." Then him again – damning all the local nobs like Esquire Hayley and then he again damns the King, again and again. I wept to hear it! He took advantage of my shocked and somewhat enervated condition, grabbed me and frogmarched me out of his garden. Frogmarched – mark that. Frenchie ways.

(*He stands.*)

I always been scared of God like they taught. I've always been loyal. I love the King. Always doffed me hat to betters. I've been beaten, imprisoned, I've spilled blood and killed – all cos I love England. Don't let this Blake bloke get away. You've got to make him an example of him, sir.

(*Darkness falls on SKOLFIELD.*)

SCENE TEN

(*A cold light dawns on* BLAKE *and* CATHERINE *shivering in the cottage.* CATHERINE *speaks as* BLAKE *raves.*)

CATHERINE: Dragged down by an aching body.

BLAKE: The charge is sedition.

CATHERINE: You seem far away.

BLAKE: Why was I born with a different face?

CATHERINE: Can't stop shivering.

BLAKE: He'll not bare opposition.

CATHERINE: Tenderness might help.

BLAKE: Hayley is Satan!

(*This snaps* CATHERINE *out of her reverie.*)

CATHERINE: You what?

BLAKE: It fits.

CATHERINE: Will…

BLAKE: He wishes me dead. He hired this soldier as agent provocateur. He'd hoped to reduce me to his lapdog and because I will not submit, he desires me hanged.

CATHERINE: Would you help me up to bed?

BLAKE: Of course.

(*He does.*) That witch Bathurst too. The whole pack of them wish me murdered…

(*They disappear up the shadowy stairs.*)

SCENE ELEVEN

(HAYLEY *and* BATHURST *sit in the false light of her drawing room.*)

BATHURST: I do not wish to be a crow, but the hermit must admit that my Jeremiads were prophetic.

HAYLEY: To what doth the lady allude?

BATHURST: Your protégé. The maniac Blake. I shuddered when confronted with his beasts and faerie fancies. I did trumpet they were products of a most deformed psyche.

HAYLEY: Surely the man's art is a matter of taste?

BATHURST: If you have taste you'll hate it! More repellent than his works are his opinions. A Republican I named him upon my – thank mercy – only encounter. This proves me veracious. This shameful episode!

HAYLEY: The soldier is a known drunkard.

BATHURST: Mister Blake is to blame.

HAYLEY: The hermit admits that Blake is a perplexing man. His views are unconventional.

BATHURST: You understate.

HAYLEY: Shortly before the incident, the hermit himself was the innocent victim of Blake's splenetic tirade. It made the hermit quite forget himself and lose his temper back.

BATHURST: You should have beat the dog!

HAYLEY: Mister Blake is no bad egg. The soldier exaggerates.

BATHURST: If even half of what he says is true, Blake merits gallows.

HAYLEY:	Mr Blake does, one fears, resemble the great Cowper in that the perilous powers of his imagination render him mentally unfit to take care of himself.
BATHURST:	Huh!
HAYLEY:	Hayley is going to hire a lawyer to help Blake in his predicament. Hayley wonders if the good Lady might contribute to the fund?
BATHURST:	It is a wonder that you wondered that.
HAYLEY:	Other well-wishers are assisting.
BATHURST:	Let others assist!
HAYLEY:	Thank you for your time in any case. The hermit wishes you a good day.
	(HAYLEY *rises*.)
BATHURST:	Are you departing?
HAYLEY:	There are some other calls to make.
BATHURST:	When will you appear again?
HAYLEY:	You wish the hermit to continue his visits despite his support for a lunatic?
BATHURST:	We must not let this small business get in the way of our society. Blake is a trifling matter. I would miss a good laugh at your jinks.
HAYLEY:	The hermit would surely miss your banter and banality.
BATHURST:	We all have our crosses to bear. If you feel you must assist this fellow…
HAYLEY:	Hayley feels for this Blake a father's love. He is Blake's patron. He cannot be deserted in his hour of need.
BATHURST:	Charity, they say, ennobles the soul.

HAYLEY: Hayley cherishes every chance to lend a hand.
BATHURST: Then Hayley's a very fine man.
(HAYLEY *bows to* BATHURST, *who smiles coquettishly. The light leaves them.*)

SCENE TWELVE

(*A cold morning light shines upon* BLAKE *and* MARY *in his garden*.)

MARY:	What have you got yerself into now?
BLAKE:	A right old pickle.
MARY:	I'll say! What'll happen?
BLAKE:	They'll hang me.
MARY:	Everyone round here knows you didn't say half them things.
BLAKE:	Tell the Jury that!
MARY:	Oughtn't you get a lawyer?
BLAKE:	Can't afford one.
MARY:	You must make things difficult.
BLAKE:	My life is cursed.
MARY:	You and me could have had a bit of fun, that's that. But no – wouldn't tell your wifey fibs so here comes this big idea of having two wives.
BLAKE:	No reason it shouldn't work.
MARY:	I ain't like her – dress ragged, eat paltry. With me, you'd have to paint my lady's screens.
BLAKE:	My refusing one job warrants such malice?
MARY:	Couldn't you have let him piss and go? You know what soldiers are like.
BLAKE:	He was a spy in the pay of your mistress and Hayley.
MARY:	Don't be daft.
BLAKE:	This is intrigue of my enemies. There'll be a carnival on the day they hang Will Blake. "Crucify him!"

MARY:	You do go on strange. Calm down. Shouting only gets you heard.
BLAKE:	I once saw Paradise in Felpham – and in you. Both places in which to hide and sleep.
MARY:	Good luck with your trial.

(*Exit* MARY. BLAKE *walks to the house and sits with his head in his hands. Enter* HAYLEY *and an ailing young lawyer,* SAMUEL ROSE.)

HAYLEY:	Here is our unfortunate plaintiff.

(BLAKE *looks up, surprised*.)

BLAKE:	Mister Hayley!
HAYLEY:	Gentle Blake – let the herm... er, me introduce you to Mister Rose.
ROSE:	Good morning, Mister Blake.
BLAKE:	How d'you do.
HAYLEY:	Rose is a very promising young lawyer. Hayl... I have engaged him as your advocate. You have need of representation, given the seriousness of the charge.
BLAKE:	That is true.
HAYLEY:	Mister Rose.

(ROSE *coughs then speaks*.)

ROSE:	I have looked over the statements of the complainant and yourself and there are discrepancies.
BLAKE:	That is because he lies, and I tell the truth.
ROSE:	His allegations have no foundation?
BLAKE:	Well, you know...

HAYLEY: Now, now! You know, good Blake, that these are times of trouble. War fever. The government panicking. Mister Rose, the same as thee and I, holds liberal views

(ROSE *coughs*.)

but not everybody shares our wish for a finer world. It is my information that your case will be heard by the Duke of Richmond. He is notoriously unloving towards Hayley.

ROSE: He might wish to make an example.

BLAKE: That I'd guessed.

(ROSE *coughs*.)

Long ago I had a vision of the giant divided Man, and my task was to show him to all. Don't you see? I shall exhibit him when my body is hung publicly, drawn, gelded, and quartered.

ROSE: They've abolished that. You'll get no more than two years with hard labour.

BLAKE: Enough to break a poet.

HAYLEY: So, when Mister Rose your advocate asks you whether you uttered any of these indiscretions, you will say to him and everyone, "the very idea!" Is that clear?

ROSE: We shall paint you as a lover of King and country.

BLAKE: I do love this country.

HAYLEY: Excellent.

(ROSE *coughs, badly this time*.)

BLAKE: Oh, Rose, thou art sick.

ROSE: Ever under the weather.

HAYLEY: Tender Rose doth often worry the Hay..., er, me.

BLAKE: Mister Hayley, I cannot deny that your generosity in this matter has come as a great surprise, seeing as at our last meeting I was somewhat froward.

HAYLEY: Desist! You embarrass the hermit. This pressing matter of getting you off is our prime concern. Mister Rose is an admirable lawyer and shall – your patron is in no doubt – win the case.

ROSE: I will endeavour.

(ROSE *coughs*.)

BLAKE: You really must take care of that chest.

ROSE: Thank you.

HAYLEY: Where is the light of your life?

BLAKE: Unhappily, my wife like Mister Rose is in ill health. She has taken to her bed.

(*A sickly little light appears upon* CATHERINE *upstairs in bed*.)

CATHERINE: A house built upon sand, my strength's sinking fast. Eroded by my shame and your irritability. I feel blamed for not being up to job of long-suffering wife. Perhaps it would be better if I died. World hates us, in any case.

(*The light fades upon her*.)

HAYLEY: Has she seen a doctor?

BLAKE: Our funds are slim.

HAYLEY: Send the bills to me.

BLAKE: You are too kind.

HAYLEY: Hayley acts from his heart. Come, Rose, let us plot legal stratagems.

ROSE: I might have to call again for information.

BLAKE:	Any time.
HAYLEY:	Anything you need, contact me.
BLAKE:	Thank you.
HAYLEY:	No need. 'Tis the hermit's mode.
	(*Exit* ROSE *and* HAYLEY.)
BLAKE:	I no longer know…
	(*Enter* MILTON.)
MILTON:	Soul, art thou lost?
BLAKE:	Have you come to gloat?
MILTON:	I?!
BLAKE:	I suppose you showed resolve in the face of death?
MILTON:	My life was in dire peril with the Stuart's restoration. I was absolute to pay the price.
BLAKE:	Weren't you at all afraid?
MILTON:	Bore it Sinai-like.
BLAKE:	I'm panic-stricken and full if nervous fear!
MILTON:	So I perceive.
BLAKE:	You didn't wish with all your might to live?
MILTON:	How can you ask? My epic was still unfinished.
BLAKE:	Mine is unfinished too. Death mocks my hopes.
MILTON:	I have a certain thing I wish to show thee.
	(MILTON *stands in the doorway. A great light begins to shine behind him.* BLAKE *stands.*)
	Come with me and glimpse true reality.
	(BLAKE *follows* MILTON *into the light as the cottage is consumed in darkness.*)

SCENE THIRTEEN

(*Coughing from the darkness. A little light comes up upon sick ROSE and HAYLEY at a table in a public house. HAYLEY's head is bandaged.*)

HAYLEY: A most calamitous happenstance! That such a thing should happen to so promising a fellow.

(*ROSE coughs and coughs and coughs. BLAKE enters with drinks.*)

BLAKE: Liberty! All thanks to your brilliant and skilled advocacy. Sweet Rose, what a great triumph you are. Thank you for hiring him, Mister Hayley. By the way, what is up with your head?

HAYLEY: The hermit nearly did not make the trial! As he was setting out to ride, his excellent domestic Miss Beke observed that her master had an old hat upon his head. She requested that he change it for a new one. The new hat proved a helmet of preservation! Later, perched upon his steed, Hayley unfurled his umbrella to shade his eyes from the glaring sun. This abrupt unfurling was followed fast by the rider being pitched forwards onto his bonce! Hayley lighted upon a flint with unusual violence. The strong shield of his new hat saved him. Some more water, frail lad?

ROSE: Thank you.

BLAKE: My trial is perhaps a first – the defence collapses and wins the case.

HAYLEY: Abstruse paradox.

ROSE: I thought at one time, in the midst of my summing up – as the worst of coughing fits seized me – that I should surely die.

BLAKE: You did a magnificent job! Your lawyer's way with words – so much for "truth" and "reality" when a fine man-of-the-bar is around.

HAYLEY: As usual for a protégé of Hayley, Rose is chief at his vocation.

ROSE: You're both too kind.

BLAKE: Not a whit. You saved my neck.

HAYLEY: Praise where praise is due.

ROSE: They never really had a case. As soon as the jury saw you, Mister Blake, standing there unafraid, eyes flashing, yelling out "false!" to Skolfield's lies, they knew who to believe, who to reject.

BLAKE: I credit you.

ROSE: You are too generous.

HAYLEY: Mister Blake, the hermit also espied your lack of fear. Yet a few weeks back, your reaction to your upcoming trial was entirely different. Why such a change, sir?

BLAKE: Sir, would you believe it: a friend showed me something which quite altered my assessment.

HAYLEY: So, Hayley's encouragement hit its usual target!

BLAKE: No, it was not your encouragement on this occasion.

(ROSE *has a coughing fit.*)

HAYLEY: Oh no?

(ROSE *drinks some water.*)

ROSE: Excuse me.

HAYLEY: What then turned your fear to fortitude?

BLAKE: I simply saw that there is no death.

HAYLEY: You speak in riddles, sir.

BLAKE: There is no death. This corporeal life is an illusion. There is no "world out there".

HAYLEY: The more Hayley considers things, the more our situation is clear. We are fortuitous atoms accidentally blessed with life. We float about on a rock in a void. Our maker, if any, is far removed. We are lost in infinite space. Time stretches forever. Dust to dust.

ROSE: I shall soon be dust.

HAYLEY: What a shame. And so promising.

BLAKE: Don't encourage him in his delusion! Of course you'll live. Disease disappears with belief. You want the feel of the Saviour's love. The only death we ever experience is that of the spirit and happily this is but a sleep.

HAYLEY: Nonsense.

BLAKE: Aye – 'tis knowledge not gained from sense experience.

HAYLEY: Blake, the hermit has done his best to help you. He will continue to employ you if and when. But you do yourself no favours with these odd, brain-turmoiled rants.

BLAKE: Well, well, time will tell.

(BLAKE *finishes his porter*.)

I have a chaise to catch.

HAYLEY: Why you had to move back to London, I'll never...

BLAKE: I did.

(*He rises*.)

Thanks for all you've done.

HAYLEY:	Ever your patron.
BLAKE:	And many thanks to you, Mister Rose.
ROSE:	I hope I did my best.
BLAKE:	Farewell, farewell, see you in London!
HAYLEY:	Farewell.
ROSE:	Farewell.
	(BLAKE *backs away from them to exit but is caught by a sudden light.*)
BLAKE:	Of a sudden I see!

(*A strange light falls upon* ROSE.)

The coughing fits quickly worsen. Your life's quality goes. I see your family worried. Your friends are losing hope. You're losing heart also. You take to bed with a pain in the chest. You bid goodbye to the law you studied. Your wracked body gives up the ghost. You're dead by seven and twenty.

(*Darkness falls upon* ROSE *as the same strange light appears upon* HAYLEY.)

You drift away from society. I hardly see you once I've left Felpham. You get a pension from the crown. Your vision worsens. You live within memories which you feel are someone else's. You cannot hold them, and the bladder pain also worsens. You die in agony alone in bed, a couple of friends only left. Hayley was once the talk of us all. Forgotten before his death.

(HAYLEY *falls into darkness.* BLAKE *stands in the light.*)

BUT THIS DOES NOT HAVE TO BE!!! If I forgive you and you forgive me, and we share that which we know. If only I could show you what was shown me a few weeks ago in the garden with Milton.

SCENE FOURTEEN

(*The light comes up on* BLAKE *who is indeed in his garden with* JOHN MILTON.)

MILTON: Soon for an end to the mystery. First, let us sort our disparities.

BLAKE: I see a falling short in you.

MILTON: What is that?

BLAKE: In how you envision God.

MILTON: What fault in my Jehovah?

BLAKE: Where to begin? A pedantic schoolmaster. A mocking, cawing, grinning and scornful, punishing, jealous and dreadfully angry old patriarch.

MILTON: These are wrongs?

BLAKE: These are the things wrong with you.

MILTON: 'Tis I you dislike?

BLAKE: I love you as a dawn full of sun. Your glorious words have flown me places from which I can take higher flights. Yours are the words have most inspired me after Christ's.

MILTON: Would you argue with Him thus?

BLAKE: Were he as full as you of errors.

(MILTON *turns, seemingly scandalized.*)

Then again, do I have you wrong? You flow with living waters of sweet truth which liberate the soul. How to square this with that countenance of stone?

MILTON: All the while I have wandered through Heaven, pondering the ways of Providence, dead though not at rest, your objections have pricked at me.

	Your way of seeing, I must confess, has imposed itself upon me. My harshness. My anger. My hatred of my enemies. I do see where 'tis they lead...

(MILTON *removes his Puritan mask.*)

BLAKE: Oh no!

(*Beneath there is* SKOLFIELD. *He shouts at* BLAKE, *who recoils.*)

SKOLFIELD: Advance with Oliver's army! Forward with pike and musket. With cutlass on horseback mew like sheaves the King's men down.

BLAKE: You!

SKOLFIELD: Just as soon for the other lot fight. Cavalier slicing new model crowns. Protestant killing Catholic. Papist slaying Calvinist. I am ever willing to lend my hand.

BLAKE: Will I never get you out of my garden?

SKOLFIELD: If it be man's work, I'll do it. Men. Women. Beasts. Babes.

BLAKE: I wish you gone!

SKOLFIELD: I am the truth behind civilisation. I keep you safe and warm in bed. I am your natural man.

(SKOLFIELD *disappears as a wind blows through the garden. The light grows dim as* BLAKE *sinks to his knees.*)

BLAKE: Fools to think anger and killing help. Our own violent spectres unchallenged. Never advancing the cause of peace. Stewing and ranting. Neglecting our loves.

(BLAKE *looks down at the ground.*)

The ground is full of creatures crawling. Running a God-forsaken race.

(BLAKE *weeps*.)

Take this cup away from me. I don't wish to go to gaol.

(*It has grown almost fully dark as* BLAKE *prays on the ground. A star appears in the night sky. A heavenly choir begins.* BLAKE *looks up to see a staircase descending. He gasps as a figure appears coming down. The light begins to rise again, beautiful, and very bright as the* LAMB OF GOD, *a beautiful, healthy, naked youth, reaches the ground. The singing of angels reaches its climax as he stands beside* BLAKE.)

Who might you be?

LAMB: Don't you know me?

BLAKE: It's as if I always have.

LAMB: Because I AM.

(*Heavenly music resounds, a crazy light show and the wind of the Spirit blows round.* LAMB *stands, arms outstretched as a shining star.* BLAKE *staggers as if his consciousness were about to explode.*)

BLAKE: You're beautiful!

LAMB: Thanks ever so.

(LAMB *capers about*.)

Some conceive of me as greybeard – but I Am Eternally young. Alive. Sparkling. Joyous. Laughing!

(LAMB *jumps and cartwheels around. The razzmatazz desists.*)

How d'you do, Man.

(LAMB *stands holding his hand out to* BLAKE. BLAKE *is on the ground, bowed.*)

Please, no need to kneel. I come as your servant. Sowing seeds to feed your hunger, stop your craving, nourish in your needs

(BLAKE *notices he is kneeling in a compromising position before* LAMB. *He springs to his feet.*)

BLAKE: Oh-my-Lord, the connotations multiply!

LAMB: Be not ashamed of any Union.

(LAMB *beams a great big smile at* BLAKE. BLAKE *laughs for joy. They hug.*)

BLAKE: It's good to have you back in my life again.

LAMB: I saw you struggling, yearning to see behind closed doors. They fly open and you see the naked truth! I am in every Man.

(LAMB *grins at* BLAKE, *who turns away ashamed.*)

BLAKE: I've been much in error. I've been a fool and got my deserts.

LAMB: I don't care fig for deserts! Yours are Mercy, Pity, Peace, and Love.

BLAKE: You'll give me these?

LAMB: Or else what hypocrisy?! I died on that cross a hopeless sinner. God-forsaken. Without any faith. We live not by punishing our brother for his mote, ignoring our beam but by forgiving each other

(*Light shines all around them.* BLAKE *laughs and* LAMB *capers.*)

BLAKE: Coming here was my mistake.

LAMB: You forgive your brother Hayley?

BLAKE:	Would I could say it to him.
LAMB:	Here you go. Talk to him.
	(HAYLEY *is there*.)
BLAKE:	Mister Hayley!
HAYLEY:	Aha! The Blake! The hermit wishes you well.
BLAKE:	I very much apologise for calling you Satan. I am that dark one.
HAYLEY:	Do not think of it again. Merely do what society expects. You have a wife to care for. Use your talents to titillate.
	(BLAKE *bristles with anger at this*.)
LAMB:	Don't lose your temper! Tell it like it is.
BLAKE:	Mister Hayley – I have been given my talents by God and I must use them as I see fit. I often feel that you are trying to bend my will to your own. I must obey my vision though you approve not. You have social position and so a certain power over me. I have worked for you, else we should have starved. If you misuse your power over me, you make honesty hard for me. Often, I have flattered to keep on your good side. I will no longer swallow my truth and ventriloquize yours. I am not for sale. I am owned by God. I trust the visions he gives me.
HAYLEY:	So it be.
	(*Exit* HAYLEY.)
BLAKE:	Now I am alone.
LAMB:	(*Attracting his attention*) Ahem!
BLAKE:	I'm never alone!
	(BLAKE *rushes to* LAMB *and falls into his arms.* LAMB *cradles* BLAKE.)

LAMB: I shall always be with thee. Hold on to your vision divine.
Go back into history and make that vision shine.
I am always here to light your way.
I do it for you. I love you, Man.
You're my friend and I'm your mate.

BLAKE: How I have missed my brother's face.

(*They embrace.* LAMB *looks into* BLAKE's *eyes.*)

LAMB: I came as a youth unto these shores.
I trod the Isle of Albion.
I founded my church upon a Tor.
That was very long ago, and I no longer have that Being.
You're living here and now. Make this world.

(*The lights, wind, heavenly choirs suddenly go mad as* LAMB *kisses* BLAKE *and one great word resounds.*)

WORD: JERUSALEM!

(LAMB *lets* BLAKE *go.* BLAKE *staggers, fighting for breath. He struggles with a line that is coming to him as* LAMB *begins to go back up the staircase.*)

BLAKE: And did...
And did those...
And did those feet...
And did those feet in
                Ancient...
                  Time...

(*As* BLAKE *struggles to articulate this vision,* LAMB *ascends and disappears from view.* BLAKE *in an ecstasy swoons.*

Darkness.

(*The morning light dawns on* BLAKE *lying in the garden as* CATHERINE *rushes from the house and comes to him.*)

CATHERINE: Will! What's the matter?

BLAKE: Matter's what we shape to create Paradise.

(*Springs to his feet and kisses her*) I love you!

CATHERINE: William! What's come over you?

BLAKE: God...

CATHERINE: Have you had of your turns?

BLAKE: Around and around!

(BLAKE *spins* CATHERINE.)

CATHERINE: Ooh-wah!

BLAKE: You look beautiful. But careworn. Have I done this to you?

CATHERINE: All I want is to be a friend to you.

BLAKE: I've been a fool.

(*They hug.*)

Here has been a mistake.

CATHERINE: It's been a ruddy great draughty pit!

BLAKE: Let's go back to London.

CATHERINE: What will Hayley say?

BLAKE: I must write.

CATHERINE: Them epic poems what no one wants to buy?

BLAKE: God provides.

(*Pause.*)

CATHERINE: What God commands we must do.

BLAKE: You comprehend?

CATHERINE: I've not lived for fifteen years with a man God visits regular without getting to know Him a bit myself.

BLAKE: His greatest miracle was sending you to me.

CATHERINE: It's a bloody bigger miracle I stay! Let's pack for London.

BLAKE: Never to look back.

(MRS BLAKE *smiles at* MR BLAKE. *They kiss. He sings his latest song to her, to a jaunty folk melody.*)

And did those feet in Ancient time
Walk upon England's mountains green?
And was the holy Lamb of God
On England's pleasant pastures seen?
And did the Countenance Divine
Shine forth upon our clouded hills?
And was Jerusalem builded here
Among these dark Satanic Mills?
(CATHERINE *joins in.*)

BLAKES: Bring me my Bow of burning gold:
Bring me my Arrows of desire:
Bring me my Spear: O clouds unfold!
Bring me my Chariot of fire.
I will not cease from Mental Fight,
Nor shall the Sword sleep in my hand
Till we have built Jerusalem
In England's green & pleasant Land.
(WILLIAM BLAKE *and* CATHERINE BLAKE *disappear into the morning light.*)

THE END

www.ingramcontent.com/pod-product-compliance
Lightning Source LLC
Chambersburg PA
CBHW021020090426
42738CB00007B/840